RESOURCING RENEWAL

Resourcing Renewal

shaping churches for the emerging future

MARTYN ATKINS

Copyright © Martyn Atkins 2007
Cover image © PureStockX

British Library Cataloguing in Publication data

A catalogue record for this book is available
from the British Library

ISBN 978-1-905958-10-8

First published by Inspire
4 John Wesley Road
Werrington
Peterborough PE4 6ZP

Typeset by Regent Typesetting, London
Printed and bound in Great Britain by
Athenaeum Press Ltd., Gateshead, Tyne & Wear

For Dennis,
a friend and brother in the Lord,
and now a member of the
Church Triumphant.

Contents

Introduction

The best time to plant a tree is twenty years ago.
The next best time is today.

African Proverb

Our love for an institution is in proportion to
our desire to reform it.[1]

John Stuart Mill

This is a book about God, and more specifically God, Father, Son and Spirit. I believe that God is the supreme missionary and evangelist. It is a book about the Church, but more precisely the Church understood as the key partner in God's mission. Even more particularly this is a book about the renewal of the Church, which I believe occurs naturally as a consequence of the Church engaging obediently and faithfully in the mission of God. Finally this is a book written by someone who has taught students about Christian mission, evangelism and church renewal for 10 years now, who loves doing that and is personally committed to what he teaches. Consequently it is not a balanced book for, in the words of Sally McFague, 'balance often qualifies insight out of existence'.[2] So this is a book with a mission as well as a book about mission!

The mission of this book emerges from my own journey as a would-be Christian disciple, pastor, teacher, and also as spouse, father and a fortunate person with many friends – both inside and outside the Christian faith. Let me explain. Increasingly I find myself to be in a place of 'in-between'. 'Inherited church' (to use a piece of shorthand that will be used throughout this book, as distinguished from 'emerging' church or 'fresh expressions') has shaped my life for over 30 years. I have led its worship, attended its (many) meetings, and shared the life of its communities. It has loved me, cared for my family and me and is even providing for my (modest) pension. I know many of its hymns word perfect and can recite by heart some of its great prayers. Most importantly it has nurtured me in faith and been the vehicle whereby I have received and tried to pursue God's call. At a deep level I love it dearly.

So naturally it is painful to realize that God's Church, God's partner in mission, to which I have committed my life and owe so much, is in dire straits in many respects. I think I understand some reasons why that is, and the following pages outline my own thinking. I could spend my time lamenting the decline and demise of inherited church, but I won't. Because what is truly wonderful – and what makes today such a fascinating time to be a Christian – is that 'fresh expressions', 'new forms of church' and the like are springing up all around. The Methodist Church in Great Britain to which I belong is declining faster than most, more 'tired' than many, and 'older' in its membership than nearly all other historic denominations. And yet, there are winds of change. For long-in-the-tooth inherited church members like me it is a time of transition, a time of in-between-ness, a time for sorting out continuity, and newness. The possibilities of further demise and deep renewal both lie open before us.

Throughout the 1990s I served on a small working group that eventually produced the *Methodist Worship Book* in 1999.[3] Not all our efforts ended up in the book itself, which is probably a good thing. For example we toyed for a long time with a (spoof) 'rite of renewal' that consisted of a single rubric: 'if there is to be a spontaneous outpouring of the Holy Spirit, it will happen here!' But this comic rite made the key point plain: renewal is fundamentally and ultimately a sovereign work of God. In that sense we cannot create it or command God to bring it about. We can't strategize or scheme in such a way that renewal *must* come. On the other hand renewal is not totally disconnected from human longing and preparation. Christians can (and must) pray for renewal, anticipate and prepare for it, in faith and hope. Nor is this a vain hope because renewal is, after all, rooted in a missionary, evangelistic, grace-giving God who desires and rejoices to make all things new. To misquote a well-known saying, 'Prepare for renewal as if it all depended on you and know that it depends completely on God.'

In this sense, then, I believe that renewal can be resourced, and this book is my modest contribution to that *desired* outcome. The first chapters deal with the nature of the Church, which I regard as essentially the gift and possession of a gracious, missionary God, and in light of this suggest that God renews the Church by its participation in God's mission. Consequently, fresh expressions of church and exciting new ministries are exactly what we should expect to experience, and long may they continue. Chapter 5 maps out some of the cultural forces that inevitably shape the environment in which the Christian Church lives and witnesses in the West today. The remaining chapters take up various themes that I consider either potentially resource renewal or hamper the possibility of renewal. I argue that those things that resource renewal require to be embraced as a matter of obedience to God, and those things that threaten to stymie the resourcing of renewal be dispensed with urgently, and an intentional, trusting openness to God be adopted. I am not expecting readers to agree with me at every point! But I am hoping that the contents will stimulate thinking and stir passion about the Church that, for all its failings, remains God's chosen, preferred vessel for embodying Jesus Christ in the power of the Holy Spirit.

As I have written this book a number of faces have never been far from my mind and they make several appearances in the following pages, both implicitly and explicitly:

- My wife, and my aged parents and parents-in-law, a big generation apart (with all that that means), but totally loyal in a variety of ways, to quite different local churches. They long for authentic renewal in themselves and the Church and, I know, often reflect upon the paucity of 'ordinary' chapel life and wonder . . .

- My three boys, now young men, none of whom shows the slightest interest in becoming a fully paid-up atheist, but two of whom show not the slightest interest in anything to do with inherited church either. One is a Christian: Bible in hand, 'WWJD' (what would Jesus do?) band on his wrist, going off each year to help lead Bible camps and Share Jesus missions, Christian music on his MP3 player, a member of the Christian Union when at university. But I know now, and I suspect it is true of very many other young Christians today, that he will probably never make the transition into inherited church.

- Some good friends, who became Christians in their mid-thirties and who now as forty-somethings are all but out of the Church: churched and almost unchurched in a decade. The reasons they cite are several and significant: church hypocrisy, self-centredness, resistance to change; the falseness and shallowness of much of what passes for Christian faith; a lack of authentic spirituality; a sense of 'not living in the real world'. Such is their perceived experience of several years in a largish, well-regarded, suburban church, a place local people would call 'a good church'. They feel deeply that 'It is impossible to be a Christian. It is impossible not to be a Christian. It is impossible to be a Christian outside the Church and the Church is impossible.'⁴ Yet they love God and are sincere and passionate about following Christ in a way that makes sense of their complicated lives.

- Some friends of the family in their fifties: lifelong members of their local churches – youth club leaders, church stewards, Bible study stalwarts. Remaining 'key members' of their local church, they confide quietly and painfully that they no longer feel they know what it is all about: the money-raising for the survival of a questionable status quo; the general level of apathy about things they consider really important; the annual round of religious routine. And yet, in a desire to become better Christians, they shared in the several-month-long Disciple course. A renewing time, but also one that has increased their sense of dis-ease with church, that sense of 'there has got to be more to it than this'. So they pray and wait.

- A number of students at Cliff College, a training college for evangelists and preachers, where I work: deeply committed Christians who are exploring a call to ordained ministry but are very wary of pursuing that path. Why? Because, although they believe God is calling them to ministry they do not easily see how their giftings, experiences and priorities can be used in inherited church. Yet the sense of God's call persists . . .

- A number of friends, who are already leaders in various denominations, ordained and lay. Sometimes confiding among each other a sickness and boredom about the routine of ministry today, but increasingly catching a sense that something is happening . . .

- Last but not least the members of the local 'pub quiz' team, to which my wife and I belong, regularly come to mind. There are about 10 of us in all and we have become good friends in recent years. We fail at the quiz regularly(!), go out for meals or watch a film together, invite each other round for grand gatherings and simple suppers alike. We laugh a lot, and at times most of us have cried and empathized with each other about sickness and sadness and children and parents and work and marriage. Three of us are regular churchgoers, and a couple more are sporadic visitors to 'hatches, matches and dispatches'. More of us went through

Sunday school than now go to church. As one member of the team said to the group recently when the topic of church came into the conversation, 'You are my church.' They possess what is common to so many people today, an antipathy and even hostility to some aspects of 'church', its life and legacy, while remaining captivated by faith, mystery, spiritual things, answered prayer, friendship, meaning, love, and Jesus Christ.

I hope and pray for them all a deeper joy and a richer faith, and a Church renewed by the Spirit and therefore reshaped for God's mission in the emerging future.

To mull over . . .

- What do you think is the balance between God's work and ours, in relation to the renewal of the Church?

- In what ways do you identify with the groups of people listed in the chapter?

1

Setting the Stall Out: Some Basic Mission Church Thinking

> Fundamentally the church exists because God through Christ and in the power of the Holy Spirit *makes* us exist – day by day, generation by generation, ever afresh.[1]
>
> *Andrew Dutney*

> Tradition isn't wearing your grandmother's hat. It's having babies of your own![2]
>
> *Nicholas Hawkes*

I can remember exactly when and where I was converted to the idea that the Church is essentially missionary in nature and purpose. It was my first church appointment as a minister and I had encouraged my devout, largely aged, congregation to have a 'lay witness weekend'. Essentially a review of local church life with a focus on renewal, it involved the visit of a number of (lay) Christians from around the country who led discussions, prayer and worship. It was Saturday morning and I joined a discussion group meeting on the disused stage in the church schoolroom on the agreed basis that, given it was a *lay* witness weekend, I didn't say anything.

'What's the purpose of our church, why are we here?' asked the leader.

'To invite people to join us' it was readily agreed.

'Yes, but why?' persisted the leader.

'Well,' said one of my stewards earnestly, 'we're all getting older and someone's got to do all the jobs – we can't go on forever.'

It was as the whole group nodded their ready assent, and I bit my tongue, that I was converted to mission-shaped church thinking.

In the beginning . . . God

Having stated that this book focuses a good deal on 'church' it may seem odd to now assert that that is the wrong starting point. But it is. Paradoxically, even when dealing with ecclesiology – material dealing with the nature of the Church – you can't properly begin at that point and, if you try, in some senses you never recover from the false start. 'One of the most important things Christians need to know about the church is that *the church* is not of ultimate import-ance.'[3] This is not to suggest that the Church is un-important, unbiblical or uninspired: quite the reverse, as I shall make clear.

Where, then, does mission-shaped thinking, even about church, properly begin? It begins with God, with theology if you like. Good thinking about church seems instinctively to understand this. Just as we cannot look at our own eyes without a mirror for reflection, so the Church cannot see itself for what it is without seeing itself via something else. Mission-shaped thinking suggests that the 'something else' is the God of mission. And not just any god, but the God revealed in the Christian Scriptures, God experienced and understood in terms of Father, Son and Holy Spirit.

Without denying the complexities of Scripture in terms of text, type, genre, form and the like, there lies in mission-shaped thinking a conviction that the meta-story of Scripture can be discerned, is deeply significant and bears witness to the fundamental character of God as missionary and evangelist.[4] So in the rich tapestry of the Old Testament is found God who creates all things, beautiful and good, who mourns broken-hearted at the spoiling of creation, and then, even as humankind signs its own death warrant in the garden, begins working for the restoration of everything and everyone. God's wooing work comes through patriarchs and prophets, matriarchs and messengers, covenants and Torah, signs and symbols. God's law is given, and God's people are rescued and led to inherit a land. Time and again they fail but God does not give them up. A new covenant is made, written on human hearts not tablets of stone. The means are many and varied and costly, but the overall aim, the mission, is plain.

In the fullness of time God, Father, Son and Holy Spirit conspire again and the crucial phase of the divine mission takes shape. Christ Jesus, God incarnate, God self-sent as it were, undertakes the missionary task of redeeming all humanity, all creation, through life laid down and resurrection glory. So the Son lives out his life making plain the nature and mission of God: teaching, healing, befriending, challenging and judging. Then God in Christ does what neither the cosmos nor humanity can do for itself: dying he destroys our death, and rising he restores our life: sacrificing, saving, rescuing.

But that is not the end. As fledgling communities of those believing in Jesus Christ are born, God again takes the initiative and comes as Holy Spirit – a missionary self-sending God in action again. Inside and outside God's new community, the Church, the Spirit comes, making bold, leading outwards, going before, preparing the way 'to Jerusalem, Samaria and to the ends of the earth.' As F.F. Bruce used to say about the book of Acts, 'It is as if God drops a pebble into the pool of human history, and we watch the ripples.' The centripetal movement of the Old Testament, with its images of nations wending their way to Jerusalem from all directions, is reversed as Pentecost becomes the launching of a centrifugal Christian mission as the Spirit impels God's people to join in and move out. The God of the Christian Scriptures – Father, Son and Spirit – is, first to last, a God of mission.

It is important to realize which way round this works. Mission-shaped thinking does not decide at the outset that God's mission comes first then scours the Scriptures to find justification for this pre-judgement. This is not an exercise in poor proof-texting. Rather, it starts from the realization that the meta-story of Scripture makes plain that God is a God of mission, that the people of God are first and foremost the *product* of God's mission, and then *participants* and *partners* in God's mission.

Seek first God's kingdom . . .

'Imitating Christ' is one of the great themes of Christian discipleship. Mission-shaped thinking takes up this theme. To share in the *missio Dei* , the mission of God or God's mission, is to imitate the missionary God as best you can. The meta-story of Scripture reveals what God is *like* by relating what God *does*. God's nature and actions agree together and combine to produce the 'shape' and 'feel' of Christian mission.

Mission-shaped thinking often presents this rich theme in terms of the pursuit of the kingdom of God. (For some, 'kingdom' language is problematic for several good reasons: tainted images of patriarchy and power, 'masculine' language, associated too closely to geography or a particular kind of national identity. Consequently, how the New Testament word *basileia* might be properly understood and applied in a globalized postmodern context is the subject of increasing interest among New Testament scholars and others. Some talk about God's 'reign' or 'rule', which addresses some of the problems of 'kingdom', but not all. Others suggest 'empire' to better articulate the alternative nature of God's new world order implied by *basileia*. For simplicity, I use 'kingdom' here, but mean by it the 'fuller sense' sought by those who seek to use alternative language to describe God's wonderful cosmic desires and designs.) If Christian mission proceeds from the revealed nature of the Trinity, then the *aim* of mission – the 'why we do it' bit, if you like – is shaped by the perceived nature of God's kingdom. The meta-story of Scripture takes us from creation to new creation, towards a time when every tear is wiped away and the Lord comes, bringing in the fullness of the reign of God. Jesus talks

13

often about his 'Father's kingdom', about seeking the kingdom first, and its coming seems to be at the heart of all he says and does. The Holy Spirit enables, inspires and calls forth witnesses to God in Christ, those who live and long for God's kingdom to come. The kingdom reign of God is the primary missional perspective of the New Testament.

We must say a little more here about the Holy Spirit in relation to the mission of the kingdom. The New Testament repeatedly makes it clear that, without the prevenient, present and permanent work of the Spirit of God, the Church cannot fulfil God's mission. 'Without the Holy Spirit,' Patriarch Athenagoras writes, 'God is far away, Christ remains a figure of the past, the Gospel a dead letter, the Church a mere organization, authority a means to exercise power, mission a propaganda machine, worship becomes outdated and morality the action of slaves.'[5] It is the Spirit who enables the appropriate incarnation and expression of Christianity for each context, place and time. It is the Spirit who calls people into ministry and service and enables them to fulfil their calling. Another kingdom theme, therefore, is a called-out people, a kingdom community that articulates and embodies these hallmarks of the reign of God. This People of God are the Body of Christ, whom they recognize and gratefully announce to be Saviour of all, regarding themselves as disciples of their Lord, believers in One who is Alpha and Omega, the beginning and the end. They are charged with the Great Commission and engage in the Great Commandment. Dying and rising, and a profound openness to the Spirit of God characterizes their life and their faith. Such a kingdom community, forged by the *missio Dei*, is the true nature of church.

God's kingdom has given shape and direction to my own mission-minded thinking and is very important to me in several respects. A focus on the kingdom offers to those seeking to be imitators of God a rich and varied mission to participate in. The imitation of the God of mission is a technicolour moving experience, not a black and white still photo. Sharing with God in bringing in the kingdom involves every facet of human life, the whole of life, in all creation. 'Thy kingdom come' may trip off the tongue easily enough, but it is a goal that fills lives and it is the ultimate goal of the Church. Such a calling rescues us from making God's mission too small, or, when we do fall into that trap, challenges us. Mission cannot properly be understood in terms of building up the 'interior' life of the church, much less numerical church growth, getting people in to 'do the jobs' or perpetuate the internal traditions of local churches. Bishop John Finney, an Anglican adviser on evangelism, once stated: 'You cannot sustain a missionary congregation. It's like a ring doughnut, there's nothing at the centre.'[6] He's right if being 'mission-minded' simply means those 'inside' being obsessed with bringing others inside who become obsessed with bringing others inside. That's less about missional ecclesiology and more about exhaustion. But when the mission is partnering God in working for the kingdom, being mission-minded is the highest and proper calling of the Church.

In my experience, however, it is not the length and breadth of the kingdom that I have felt the need to promote most. Rather, it is active witness, faith-sharing, proclamation, and being deliberate and intentional about making more followers of Jesus Christ that need bringing to centre stage. These somehow quickly become 'optional extras' rather than the core kingdom activities they are, and as such cannot legitimately be excluded. Also, although the kingdom is not to be confused with the life of the Church, participating in God's mission and pursuing the kingdom inevitably results in Christian communities being formed and thereby 'church' appears. Kingdom and church are umbilically connected, but in mission-minded terms it is important to get the connection right.

Taken together, these checks and balances serve to keep the focus on the kingdom and therefore on the essentially missionary nature of the Church. To quote Howard Snyder:

> The church gets into trouble whenever it thinks it is in the church business rather than the Kingdom business. In the church business, people are concerned with church activities, religious behavior and spiritual things. In the Kingdom business, people are concerned with Kingdom activities, all human behavior and everything God has made, visible and invisible. Kingdom people see human affairs as saturated with spiritual meaning and Kingdom significance. Kingdom people seek first the Kingdom of God and its justice; church people often put church work above concerns of justice, mercy and truth. Church people think about how to get people into the church: Kingdom people think about how to get the church into the world. Church people that the world might change the church; Kingdom people work to see the church change the world. When Christians put the church ahead of

the Kingdom, they settle for the status quo and their own kind of people. When they catch a vision of the Kingdom of God, their sights shift . . . If the church has one great need, it is this: To be set free for the Kingdom of God . . .[7]

Then the Church . . .

Such is the symbiotic relationship between God's character, God's reign, God's mission and God's Church that already it has been impossible to narrate the nature of one without reference to the others. However, having focused on the nature of God and the goal of God's kingdom, we can now focus on the nature of the Church more closely as we have created the proper theological context for such a discussion. The Church derives its being from the missionary God and is created and shaped to share in the *missio Dei*, the goal of which is the coming of the kingdom. David Bosch writes, 'The classical doctrine on the *missio Dei* as God the Father sending the Son, and God the Father and the Son sending the Spirit was expanded to include yet another "movement": Father, Son and Holy Spirit sending the church into the world.'[8] We see much this same movement in Scripture: 'As the Father sent me,' says Jesus, 'so I send you.'[9] In this way the Christian Church derives its life, nature, mission and ministry from God. Whatever God is perceived to be like, the Church, if it is true and faithful, will embody and emulate. If God is encountered and experienced as supreme missionary, going before, searching out, inviting and receiving in, abiding with, then those very characteristics will be found in the Church of such a God. If God is known as One who is always self-giving, and urging and bringing *shalom*, then so will the Church be, and so on. The true nature of the Church is determined by its creator. The Church therefore 'does not "have" a mission; it is mission. There is one trinitarian people . . . that reflects the one God who is lover, beloved and love itself . . . one God who is sender, sent and sending.'[10] Church thus becomes the vehicle of God's mission, itself infilled and impelled by the Sender Sent and Sending One. This turns on its head some of the earlier models of mission theology, all of which were variations that began talk about mission with talk about church.

It is important to note here some ramifications of this basic conviction about the (derived) nature of church, which are major themes of this book – explicit and implicit.

- It is vital to realize that the Church is not relegated in significance when understood in this way. Indeed it might be argued that the Church only finds its true significance when it understands itself as chosen and sent by God, sharing in God's mission, and without such an understanding the Church lacks ultimate identity, meaning or purpose.

- It means that the Church is the normative mission agency of a missionary God. It is divinely created as such. We might baulk – as many of us do – about the seeming non-missionary, unevangelistic nature of much church as we know it today, of its current nominality and ineffectiveness. We might assert – as many of us do – that church must change to more closely resemble its role in God's missional intentions. What we cannot do – which some mistakenly try to – is to go about the business of mission and evangelism as if the Church was some optional extra and can be bypassed. Churchless mission and missionless church are equally unsatisfactory. Whatever works of grace our wonderful God brings about always results in fresh expressions of church. We might remain open to be persuaded about some current expressions of church, but we cannot conceive of the *missio Dei* without 'church'.

- Church derived from the *missio Dei* means that whenever church and mission in pursuit of the kingdom are not synonymous, things can be said to be wrong. It is no accident that the Pentecost event marks not only the 'birthday' of the Church but also the 'birthday' of the Christian mission. So, whenever mission is relegated or supplanted as the essential defining characteristic of church, things are deemed to be amiss and incomplete. Church defined by the *missio Dei* never finds its true centre by looking in on itself. For example, whenever preoccupation with its own survival takes centre stage then church is deemed to have ceased to live in harmony with its very life-force, lost sight of its *raison d'être* and inevitably dysfunction and atrophy sets in. Lesslie Newbigin commented, 'When the church ceases to be a mission, then she openly denies the titles by which she is adorned in the New Testament.'[11]

- Church understood and defined missiologically implicitly critiques all other understandings of church. Missional church is the lens in the camera, no matter what pictures are taken, and as such there are implications for all other conceptions and understandings about the nature, life, shape and practices of the Christian Church in the sense that they are evaluated by this primary missiological understanding. Generally speaking, missiologists have been scathing of ecclesiologies in which the Church focuses in upon itself, or appears to conceive its nature or purpose independent of the *missio Dei*. They have tended to associate such defective ecclesiology with times when the Church has been, or assumed itself to still be, in a Christendom mode in the broadest sense. Hoekendijk, a particularly acerbic critic, put it like this: 'Ecclesiology has been a subject of major concern only in the "*second* generation"; in the "first generation", in periods of revival, reformation or missionary advance, our interest was absorbed by christology, thought-patterns were determined by eschatology, life became a doxology and the Church was spoken of in an unaccented and to some extent rather naïve way . . .'.[12] David Bosch talks about 'second generation' ecclesiology developing 'a weight of its own'[13] a logical consequence of theological thinking about the *Church itself* divorced from missiological moorings. While a more rounded ecclesiology than Hoekendijk would permit will be advocated in this book it remains the case that, generally speaking, churches that are growing and developing at various points around the globe are not often associated with spending time on complex, precise ecclesiologies. And those denominations that issue long, highly nuanced, beautifully crafted and perfectly balanced statements of perceived self-identity are not, generally speaking, those which are growing – in terms of either size or vitality.

- Church as the primary partner of the missionary God explains why fresh expressions arise at all. They are not, as some assert, some aberration or simply an expression of maverick selfishness or discontent. At best they are expressions of a missionary God raising up a people who can effect God's highest intentions and deepest desires for this time and place. Put sharply, if the *missio Dei* in any time and place cannot be pursued with the Church as it is, God raises up a new Church.

- All this is, essentially, the proper nature of renewal and is the primary way in which renewal is understood throughout this book. Put simply, renewal comes about when the Church takes its place in the mission of God in pursuit of the kingdom, and opens its life so as to become one with the God of mission. Obedience to God through openness to the Holy Spirit of mission takes precedence over all other factors in terms of the life and role of the Church.

For those like myself, who have been converted to mission-mindedness, this theological framework for locating and understanding the nature and function of Church is crucial. The Christian God of mission first – the kingdom of God on earth as it is in heaven as the purpose – the Church as partner in the mission, being renewed by the mission – in that order. What a marvellous guide and shaper for the witness, worship and general life of church, whether locally, regionally, nationally or globally! What a wonderful promise of renewal!

Of course, the real challenge of mission-minded thinking about church is turning thinking into reality. It isn't easy. 'Church for church's sake' is a temptation common to very many congregations today, and even when the rhetoric is missionary, outward and king-dom-orientated, church life lived out often signals different priorities. 'Churchcentredness' is so subtly seductive precisely because it arises naturally out of commitment, caring and generosity. It is a harsh and ironic reality that sheer investment over many years makes church folk susceptible to automatically assum-ing that the routine life and ministry of the local church *is* seeking the kingdom, and that keeping the 'show on the road' *is* sharing in the mission of God. And it is because this temptation is so common and so debilitating to renewal that the missionary nature of the Church requires to be rehearsed and reviewed over and over again.

One of the reasons I am enthusiastic about fresh expressions of church – whether emerging out of inherited church structures or not – is that mission-mindedness and shapedness and renewal are so often clearly evident in them. Indeed, one of the 'prompts' resulting in a 'fresh expression' is often a sense of call or vision experienced by a few Christians to 'go' rather than to invite folk to 'come'. For example, this is a prominent and repeated theme of the churches featured in the *Fresh Expressions* DVD and 'expres-sions' newspaper. Many a 'pub church' and 'café church' have begun in this way. One of the best means of renewing and energizing inherited congregations I know is prayerfully to revisit the missionary nature of the Church and deliberately develop an authentic, contextually apt fresh expression of church. After all, making babies is more fun than building coffins!

To mull over . . .

- How do you react to the statement 'the Church is not of ultimate importance'? How do you respond to it?

- Using some central stories and themes of the Bible, how is God revealed as a 'missionary, evangelist God'?

- To what extent is the life and ministry of your local church 'kingdom orientated'?

- If the 'Church is the normative agency of a missionary God' how is your local 'agency' faring in mirroring the chief characteristics of God?

- 'One of the best means of renewing and energizing inherited congregations I know is prayerfully to revisit the missionary nature of the Church and deliberately develop an authentic, contextual, apt fresh expression of church.' Spend some time rehearsing some possible fresh expressions of your church. How can you help your church move from thinking to doing?

2

More Mission-shaping Thinking about Church

Ecclesiology assumes greater urgency in times of conflict or renewal in the Church as old beliefs and structures are placed under strain [1]
Paul Avis

It's life Jim, but not as we know it . . .
(apparently *never* said by Spock to Captain Kirk in the original *Star Trek* series!)

For some readers the previous chapter will be quite enough! They will skip over this material without incurring any serious harm. Other readers will desire – some will even need, for a variety of reasons – more material relating to the theological assertion that the essential nature and purpose of the Church is missionary. This chapter, like the previous one, represents a personal journey of faith because my thinking about church has evolved over the years. My Ph.D., many years ago, focused on sacramental theology and this led me to own, at least for a Methodist, a relatively 'high' view of church and its worship life that has never left me. As part of my research I read lots of 'classic' ecclesiology (ecclesiology being the doctrine of the nature of the Church). The nature of the Church was spoken for through ancient credal statements like 'one holy catholic and apostolic', it was made clear through formal and liturgical texts, and configured around offering God rightful praise and worship. My conversion to mission-shaped church thinking has not always sat easily with this material, but being reluctant to move to an either/or situation I now realize I have been shaped by my commitment to both classic and 'missional' emerging ecclesiology. The latter is the focus here, but the former keeps rightly nuzzling in.

Why think about the Church at all?

In a time of proliferating 'fresh expressions', 'new ways of being church' and 'emerging churches' it is vital to consider the issue of the nature of church. Vital, I think, for several reasons. First, it is significant how many contemporary books explore and describe 'fresh expressions' and the like without any explicit reference to ecclesiology at all. They write as if no one else has ever before reflected on the nature of the Church or, if they have, produced nothing worth rehearsing. Just why this is the case is not always clear, but is not unimportant. Such writers remind me of those who love to see a busy garden in bloom but have no real interest in what the plants and flowers are called or, indeed, which are flowers and which weeds. Just let it all grow! Second, it is equally significant how many books focus upon and explore ecclesiology without any apparent recognition or awareness that 'fresh expressions' are emerging all around them. As a result, the doctrine of the Church they so painstakingly define appears 'wooden' and theoretical, unrelated to the many expressions of *ecclesia* springing up. These writers remind me of those who have colour co-ordinated, genus-specific window boxes, where nothing can grow unless it is first approved then long cultivated. There are sources that span this gap, of course, but not many, which is another reason for identifying a few sources here that have helped me along the way.

But there is also a pastoral reason for including some ecclesiological material here. I am privileged to know a number of pastors and leaders in 'fresh expressions' and overall, for what it is worth, they impress me deeply. Generally speaking they deal faithfully and honestly with situations that are not only exciting but also messy and unpredictable. They encounter more than their fair share of criticism and vilification – from both inside and outside their de-nominations and/or congregations – while retaining a great capacity for humour and life and joy. Most emerging church leaders I know are faithfully fragile rather than imperiously imperial. They seem to me to be more concerned about being disciples than being mavericks. They are fully aware of their own frailties and inadequacies as well as those of their congrega-tions. Consequently the question 'But is it church?' posed to their own fresh expressions exercises these church leaders deeply.

A provisional mission-shaped ecclesiology

I want to take up here some themes implicit in the previous and following chapters. My own ecclesio-logy – a work in progress, which is effectively what is outlined here – emerges when several pieces of related input are taken together cumulatively.

- *Mission-shaped ecclesiology enjoys a love-hate relationship with 'traditional' understandings of the Church.*

As a lover of Christian history and not naturally icono-clastic, it means a lot to me that Christian leaders prayed long and deliberated hard at famous Councils, and came to declare, in a phrase made immortal by the formulations of classic Creeds, that the Church was 'one holy catholic and apostolic'. Even today these 'marks' –as they are often known – are taught to those undergoing preparation for confirmation or membership. The Church has an inherent unity in Jesus Christ. Therefore in spite of many visible signs to the contrary there is, theologically can only be, one Church. Because this *one* Church is God's idea and is the Body of Christ (a phrase closely associated with Holy Communion, which is no accident) it is *holy*. This one holy Church is universal and worldwide, and that, Protestants particularly are told, is the proper rendering of the term *catholic*. This one holy catholic Church is governed and ordered by leadership which participates in, and therefore continues, the ministry of Christ's own Apostles. In this sense the Church is *apostolic*.

Alongside this rightful honouring of attributes declared to be 'the faith of the Church' has come about a growing realization that they did not simply drop out of heaven, but, rather, emerged in a particu-lar context for particular reasons. It was Cyprian, an early Christian leader who, for a number of good local, political and theological reasons, urged their adoption as sound teaching and aspirations for a somewhat fraught local church situation, but what followed is more problematic. Applied later by different people in different times and situations 'one holy catholic and apostolic' became synonymous with the medieval western Catholic Church, which was itself virtually synonymous with the Holy Roman Empire. This is the era in which Cyprian's famous quotation *extra ecclesiam nulla salus* ('outside the Church there is no salvation') became less an incentive to gospel mission and more a threat of the consequences of ecclesiastical exclusion. Liturgically this is marked by prayers for the unsaved changing from expressions that such people are in *need* of the gospel to assertions that they are in *error* of true faith. Luke's parable of the feast in which the master tells his servants to 'go to the highways and byways and compel them to come in' is used to suggest that mission in this time is often characterized by coercion and compulsion. As a result the way the Church understands itself moves away from critical examination and evaluation and towards self-righteous congratulation.

Whether talking to other Christians (particularly those in the East), or arguing with those deemed to be heretics, or contending with Jews and Muslims, the Church based primarily in Rome automatically identified itself as the one holy catholic and apostolic Church. 'One' came to mean 'this one' and suffered no real alternatives. This one alone was holy and catholic, nor did any other possess leadership in the true succession of the apostles. What was initially a statement of witness and a challenge to piety became, at its worst, a piece of ecclesiastical apartheid. None of this makes the four classic marks *wrong* in themselves, but it does mean that they have not only been used but also abused. They are not, for mission-minded folk like me, neutral, exhaustive or unquestionably applied in the same way for all time.

Of course, assessing the 'four marks' is nothing new. Working out the true nature of the Church was virtually an obsession of the Protestant Reformers of the sixteenth century. The reason is understandable. Is it possible to part from the body that claims to be the one true Church and remain properly church? Can you define and express yourself differently to that ecclesial body while still asserting that you are *truly* 'church'? Pursuing the cause that this was not only possible but also crucial brought about more classic ecclesiology.

The Reformers' response was threefold. First, they affirmed key aspects of inherited ecclesiology, such as one holy catholic and apostolic. It was not to be abandoned as merely Roman Catholic. Second, however, they went to great lengths to identify and explain where their interpretation of these historic marks differed from what they perceived the Catholic understanding to be. They did this by turning to the Scriptures as their rule and guide, and this, thirdly, led them to identify new 'marks', which as far as they were concerned also properly constituted 'church'. True church required that 'the word' be faithfully preached, that (a reduced number of) sacraments be rightly administered and that 'godly discipline' prevailed. Some of their writing was deeply moving. Luther wrote, 'The holy Christian people are externally recognised by the holy possession of the sacred cross. They must endure every misfortune and persecution, all kinds of trials and evil from the devil, the world, and the flesh . . . by inward sadness, timidity, fear, outward poverty, contempt, illness, and weakness, in order to become like their head, Christ.'[2] Such language expresses a quite different ecclesiological mood to that sometimes associated with one holy catholic and apostolic, and one much more appealing to missional ecclesiology.

Assessing classic, inherited ecclesiology continues today, not least by those committed to mission-minded thinking. Fresh expressions of church inevitably mean that many Christians today are seeking to determine whether this or that emerging model can be regarded as truly church and seeking criteria whereby that can be ascertained.

I hold the view that the four classic marks of church are not in error or irrelevant, but equally are neither exhaustive nor comprehensive. Howard Snyder retains the four classic marks of one holy catholic and apostolic but holds alongside them four 'mirror' marks that, though not explicitly found in creeds, have always been present in Christianity. Alongside *one* (emphasizing uniformity) the church is *diverse* (emphasizing variety). Alongside *holy* (emphasizing 'apartness') the church is *charismatic* (emphasizing 'anointedness'). Alongside *catholic* (emphasizing universality) the church is *local* (emphasizing contextuality). And alongside *apostolic* (emphasizing authority) the church is *prophetic* (emphasizing 'sentness').[3] In this way classic marks of church are retained but reworked in a way that makes clear that the Church is not only an organized institution but also an organic movement.

- *Mission-shaped ecclesiology prefers 'bottom-up practical' rather than 'top-down perfect' church thinking.*

Whether deriving from Cyprian or Luther the classic ecclesiologies of the previous section are both now considered 'top-down' in nature, even if their origins lie in reflecting upon a real context and situation. While appreciating such material, many mission-minded thinkers find they are drawn to ecclesiology that begins from the ground up. Top-down ecclesiology is perceived to be non-functional. It seems to stymie rather than enable the pursuit of the mission-ary nature of the Church in the world.[4] Impressive logic and theological reasoning is used to produce a doctrine of a perfect church. But such an ideal church appears to have no recognizable counterpart here in the 'real world', and this lack of realism has become an increasingly negative factor to mission-minded thinkers when reflecting on the nature of the Church.

Two writers in particular have influenced my own 'bottom-up practical' thinking about the Church, one a European Protestant, the other a South American Catholic, which itself is significant. The first is the great German pastor and theologian Dietrich Bonhoeffer. Criticism about top-down ecclesiology pre-dates Bonhoeffer; for example, it is in evidence at all the great missionary councils from Edinburgh 1910 onwards. But it was Bonhoeffer's writing about church in several places that marked a sea change in my own thinking and it thrilled my heart as I read it. He was clearly aware of top-down ecclesiology and respectful of it in its own terms. However, he considered that it created a chasm between what church is (the perfect ideal) and what church is (the stark reality) and this neutered the Church's missionary nature and role in the world. He suggested that there was a point at which the sheer unattainablilty of 'perfect church' depressed rather than encouraged Christians, and resulted in resignation rather than resolution that such a church can be attained this side of heaven. Bonhoeffer's own ecclesiology was certainly challenging, but not 'unattainable' in that sense. His church was essentially 'down on earth' rather than 'up in heaven'. He was concerned most with real church in a real world. As a mission-minded evangelical, so was I! I was aware I had a fundamentally different theology of mission to his at various points and that he had been dead for decades. Nevertheless, reading Bonhoeffer convinced me that 'top-down perfect' thinking about church was mission-fatiguing, and seeking real church in a real world was mission-inspiring.

Bonhoeffer convinced me, but it was reading Leonardo Boff's *Ecclesiogenesis*[5] that converted me to the value of bottom-up church thinking. The sub-title of the book 'The Base Communities Reinvent the Church' said it all. Boff, a Brazilian Franciscan, took on each critical question levied at these reinvented churches, and made a compelling case which crucially, at least as far as I was concerned, demonstrated that new ways of understanding church were both proper and possible. Base communities were a reaction to, and rejection of, the organizational form and heavily hierarchical framework of inherited western church. They were very different from 'proper church' but were nonetheless properly church. They were God-impelled, Christ-bearing and Spirit-led, 'a renaissance of very church'. And because they were new they created their own categories of self-expression, generated a new ecclesiology. This, Boff argued, was inevitable because the history of the Church was a 'genuine history', meaning that the Church lived in a situation of 'never-before-experienced novelty' rather than a 'return to the pristine experiences of the historic past'. Ever since the New Testament, he argued, the Church has been 'a pluriform institutional incarnation of the faith'[6] and base communities represent another such model. Boff's apologetic cemented a critically important basic building block of missional ecclesiology into my thinking. Church could be very different from inherited models and could still legitimately be church – in both God's eyes and human eyes alike.

The missiological significance of 'bottom-up' rather than 'top-down' understandings of church must not be underestimated. Ronald Inglehart notes that by 1997, in countries throughout the world, with hugely different cultural backgrounds and levels of modernization, the level of active, self-determined engagement by Christian churches of all types has grown. He writes: 'It appears that, almost across the board, certainly with a degree of agreement not often seen in our fragmented world, top-down models of everything are being increasingly challenged, and renewal is increasingly being sought from below, from the grass roots.'[7]

- *Mission-shaped ecclesiology asserts that 'church' is bigger and broader than it is often presented or conceived.*

This aspect of my conversion to missional ecclesiology has arisen not so much through reading books but by meeting Christians in various places around the world. You simply cannot visit Christians in Sierra Leone, in the wake of the terrible war of recent times, and share in their worship and witness, without being totally convinced you are 'in church'. Yet they have so little and in certain respects conform to so few 'rules' that serve to define and declare 'church' in my homeland and tradition. Similarly, a recent visit to Cuba was simply mind-blowing. Liturgical practices that would make your hair curl; sound systems that blew your ears out; a 'sanctuary' akin to an allotment shed; leadership that is almost entirely lay and (at least as far as European standards would suggest) largely untrained. But there I found a mixture of passion and grace and fellowship and care that I have never found before. And what dancing! You just know it's church. It's not so much 'where there is church, there is Christ', but more 'where Christ is, there is the church'.

But this is not all that is meant when I talk about missional thinking about church being bigger and broader. There is more to it than recognizing and accepting that Christians worship differently and occupy different kinds of physical spaces when they do so. Fundamentally this issue is about the relationship of the 'church' and 'the world'. In recent years the writer who has put this most powerfully into my own head is Filipino theologian Melba Maggay. Drawing upon the work of Dutch philosopher, Herman Dooyeweerd, she makes a distinction between the church regarded 'as the focus of a faith community's liturgical and sacramental life, and the church regarded as a community spread out in visible witness in all areas of life.'[8] The visible church is not simply congregations meeting in certain places, nor is it the church only when it is at worship. Rather, the visible church in its broadest sense 'embraces all the structures of our temporal human existence'.[9] Movements of God in schools, businesses and governments are just as much churches, parts of the body of Christ, bearing witness to the Lordship of Christ over all human structures. One significant result of this broader definition is that for Maggay the distinction between 'church' and 'parachurch' institutions appears somewhat artificial and a product of what she calls 'clerico-centred' thinking. Indeed, a number of mission church thinkers have observed that, by such criteria, many of our inherited and present models of church are in fact 'non-church', and some models historically regarded as 'un-church' 'sub-church' or 'parachurch' are, by such criteria, much more truly church than we have admitted.[10]

The images Maggay chooses to illustrate this under-standing of church bear mentioning. Church is the 'city on a hill', a community created as a signal of God's chosen way to change the world and each human being in it. Church incarnates the gospel of liberation, by which is meant not 'mere developmental-ism', delivering social service programmes and health care. Rather, such church imitates Jesus, who empties himself, becomes humanly vulnerable and suffers the deprivations of human conditions. Church, therefore, 'dwells' as profoundly as it is able without – and with-out necessarily seeking – the benefit of cultural, social or educational baggage. Only such a church enables parity and partnership, avoids paternalism, and pre-vents people from being reduced to objects of charity.

All this stands in stark contrast to many strands of inherited western ecclesiology, but I find it compelling and winsome. More than this I consider it prophetic in relation to church in the West and its dogged Christendom ecclesiologies. This bigger and broader thinking about church, which is not uncommon in the communities of 'developing world' Christianity – both among many persecuted minority churches and exploding renewed churches alike – judges and challenges the dominant ecclesiologies of the western churches. For, in spite of its rhetoric about living in 'Christian cultures', western ecclesiology mainly con-tains faith within the walls of a church and implicitly rejects the idea that being Christian shapes the every-day behaviour and witness of the believer in the whole of life. Rejecting what Mark Greene calls the 'sacred secular divide'[11], that is, the tendency of the western Church to narrow the religious life into the 'private' and divorce sacred and secular, Maggay writes, 'Historically, the church has been a genuine, alternative centre of power when it has been most aware and conscious of who it is and to whom it belongs . . . Its power comes from above. It belongs to a king and a kingdom which do not derive their power from this world and its forces.'[12]

There is one more example of 'bigger and broader' ecclesiology being better that I want to mention here. Quite a lot of ecclesiological material I read seems not only dominated by a too narrow *definition* of church, but also a preoccupation with the idiosyncrasies of a particular denomination or tradition. In this way the *polity* of this denomination or that becomes dominant, often at the cost of much bigger and broader ecclesiological themes. Ecclesiology by denominational distinctiveness; 300 pages of why X denomination is as it is! As a result, by comparison with the profound and prophetic ecclesiology of people like Maggay this stuff appears domestic, self-absorbed and increasingly irrelevant in our western post-Christian context. Inside the world of church, in an ecumenical age when denominational churches are anxious to define themselves very carefully for good motives of working together or strengthening common witness, material of this kind is understandable. Nevertheless its very myopia irritates rather than stimulates mission-minded thinkers, for whom bigger and broader ecclesiological themes are regarded more relevant and ultimately more necessary and significant. In short, much 'inherited' ecclesiology simply lives on too small a map!

- *Mission-shaped ecclesiology gives two and a half cheers for church thinking emerging from the missionary/ecumenical movements.*

The twentieth century is often referred to – at least by western Christians – as the 'ecumenical century' and it is well known that the 'ecumenical movement' arose out of the Protestant missionary movement of the nineteenth century. Mission and ecumenism, then, share a history that, it might be imagined, results in mission-minded thinkers being naturally committed to ecumenism. Yet this is a complex relationship of many nuances and sub-groups. Why is it that mission-minded church thinkers regard ecumenism as a mixed blessing at best?

The main reason is that neither the missionary nor the ecumenical movements have *fully* produced the ecclesiological thinking or missional models sought by mission-minded thinkers who are seeking a way forward today. At the heart of mission-shaped ecclesiology is the conviction that the *Church*, in a multitude of expressions, is essentially missionary in nature and character. Such thinking can be found in much ecumenical literature, but is dogged somewhat because of the historic division between mission and church. The huge Protestant missionary activity of the nineteenth century came not through churches directly, but indirectly through their mission *societies*. Those called to overseas mission were, to be sure, usually members of local churches but were selected and sent to their destinations by a mission society. Once there, for a number of reasons, they were not encouraged – indeed were often actively discouraged – from regarding their mission camps or stations as 'churches'. Back in Britain, or wherever, denominations raised huge sums of money to support the mission work, but the work itself was done through a missionary 'arm'. Perhaps such organizational apparatus was inevitable, but the result was that mission became conceived as (a) done somewhere else, (b) by those individuals who felt a special call to 'that kind of thing', (c) via an organization through which the churches 'outsourced' such activity, (d) the aim of which seemed to be about spreading Christianity without permitting 'churches' as normally understood to arise. Churches did arise over time, of course, but it cannot be said, generally speaking, that missionary societies quickly or enthusiastically enabled or encouraged this to happen. Much more time and effort was spent asserting and demonstrating that missions were not churches and churches were not missions. In this way, what mission-shaped ecclesiology necessarily holds together is here kept apart, ensuring that the resulting ecclesiology is fundamentally flawed as a result.

As the missionary movement melded into the ecumenical movement, a transmutation occurred, beginning in earnest at the Missionary Conference in Edinburgh in 1910. 'Churches' rather than 'missions' moved to centre stage, a conscious corrective of the previous separation of one from the other. In a fraught air of wariness and optimism the International Missionary Council moved through several stages of transformation to become the World Council of Churches (WCC). Aspirations and intentions that had been put on hold as World War II wrecked Europe and beyond were dusted down, sobered and sharpened up by the War itself, then quickly reshaped so that by 1948 the modern ecumenical movement was well and truly born. But by the 1960s some of the main constituent parties of the WCC were uneasy partners. A 'euthanasia of mission' was called for. Evangelical Christians, who had probably invested most in the missionary activities of the past, felt that an evangelistic impulse was being progressively rejected by what was regarded as a powerful evolving liberal consensus of the WCC, and as a result formed their own covenants throughout the world of evangelical Christianity.[13] Whether wholly justified or not, there was a widespread perception that 'church' had parted company from 'mission' in a crucial evangelistic sense. Consequently, although enormous amounts were written about both church and mission, and a good deal of it *contributes* to missional ecclesiology, the intrinsic interconnection of mission and church is not made to satisfaction in historical ecumenical material. In more recent times WCC material has certainly begun to recapture a holistic mission which explicitly includes *evangelistic* mission, but the spectre of a theologically liberal ecclesial consortium is hard to erase.

Of course, for most Christians today ecumenism is not encountered at this global level, but at local or sometimes national level. In terms of local people joining together in a common purpose of witness, mission and service, ecumenism lies easily with some of the central convictions of mission-shaped ecclesiology and I readily acknowledge that here. But in other ways it does not. There is a nagging perception in many involved in fresh expressions of church today – justified or not – that ecumenism by inherited denominations makes monolithic what should be multicoloured, that in spite of the repeated rhetoric of 'unity not uniformity', a concern with 'form' and 'order' dominates practical engagement in mission and evangelism, and that its aims, whether they be

articulated in the 'visible union' schemes of yester-
year or the partnerships and covenants of today, all
fall foul of a certain kind of 'fiddling while Rome
burns' irrelevance in the context of an increasingly
post-Christian Europe. I was leading worship at a
'new church' and during the 'notices' the pastor made
an impassioned plea for members to accompany him
in attending the 'Week of Prayer for Christian Unity'
service at the local parish church that evening. A
more open, encouraging soul it would be hard to find
and one totally committed to a number of wonderful
projects in the area. 'I can't get them to join in these
formal occasions,' he said later. Then he added, 'Can't
say I blame them, it is a low point in my calendar too.
All talk and no action.' Such church leaders are not
'anti-ecumenical' as much as instinctively convinced
that the kingdom of God involves going beyond, even
breaking down, the boundaries of classic ecumenical
thinking, which seem to be unhelpfully trapped within
the institutions and functions of inherited church.

I recall taking an informal 'straw poll' among
ordained ministers I met in the various church circles
in which I move. It was around the time that the
Church of England and the Methodist Church were
expressing a mutual commitment to mission and ministry, which in time has become a formal Covenant
relationship.[14] Though by no means a 'proper study'
– just a few dozen acquaintances chatting, really – a
pattern of three broad groupings was discernible. The
first group were those thrilled at the prospect of a(ny)
new opportunity that might bring Christian denominations closer together. They tended to be older, those
who could remember the disappointment of previous
ecumenical 'schemes', and who clearly regarded any
ecumenical step forward coming about in the remain-

ing years of their active ministry as an answer to long-made prayers. The second group, without being intrinsically critical of ecumenism, were more wary. A repeated view went something like this: 'Covenant, fine. Nice to see mission as an aim, makes a lot of sense. But if it starts to get bogged down in matters about recognizing each other's ordination, or who can take Communion in which churches, then I have no time for it. I can't bear the thought of the next 10 years of my ministry being dominated by things like that. Let's just get on with it.' Overall this 'pragmatic' view was the most prominent. The third group tended to be those who had been in ordained ministries the shortest time and also tended to be the youngest in years. To them such formal ecumenical developments were 'nice' but essentially irrelevant to how they saw their ministry unfolding. They held in tension two themes. They were more confident about their own denominational identity and about the value of this identity to the missionary nature of the whole Church than were the other groups. At the same time they recognized that they live in a post-denominational age rather than an ecumenical age. As a result they were more 'naturally' ecumenical in term of actually working with 'whoever' in common causes, both evangelistic and social justice in nature. It was missional rather than primarily ecumenical ecclesiology that fired their minds and hearts.

While probably more classically ecumenically minded than many committed to fresh expressions today I confess to having some sympathy with these views. I remember the impact Lesslie Newbigin's *The Household of God*[15] made upon me. Here was someone steeped in mission and committed to international ecumenism writing passionately about church but not advocating the kind of woolly 'melting pot' theories that critics found so useful in order to dismiss all ecumenical notions. Instead, in three masterly overviews of biblical themes, Newbigin suggested that the Church, *The Household of God*, was best articulated as *the congregation of the faithful*, *the body of Christ* and *the community of the Holy Spirit* strands. These in turn he identified broadly as Protestant, Catholic and Pentecostal[16] ecclesial traditions, all of which needed the others to function properly and coherently. One could not say to the other 'I have no need of you' because, given the needs of the world, each tradition was needed to be itself. Indeed, Newbigin implied that, rather than the historic splits between Christian traditions being regarded merely as unmitigated disasters to be put right as a first priority, or the explosion of denominations seen as a crime to be rectified as quickly as possible, God was able to take the various strands of Christianity and use them all in the salvific purposes of the *missio Dei*. It is for reasons such as these that mission-shaped ecclesiology regards some classic ecumenical thinking and modelling as a mixed bag.

- *Mission-shaped ecclesiology prefers images of church to definitions of church*

As has already been demonstrated missional ecclesiology tends to use and value the variety of imagery used in the New Testament in relation to church rather than more fixed definitions of church. The way the New Testament deals with the nature and functions of the *ecclesia* is vital to many involved in fresh expressions. Not only does Scripture seem to give permission for fluid rather than fixed 'church talk' and the bigger and broader notions of church outlined earlier, but being *Scripture* its images take precedence over the four classic 'marks' on the grounds of both antiquity and authority. This may be one reason why so much fresh expression material bypasses most 'classic' ecclesiology.

The sheer number and variety of *Images of the Church in the New Testament* becomes clear to any reader of Paul Minear's classic book of that title[17] where dozens of images are laid out and expounded. The Church is *the people of God, the body of Christ, servant, bride, vineyard, flock, household, building* and many more. Some of these images are used to describe fresh expressions of church. For example the rise of 'house' churches and church in homes; the notion of 'vineyard' to describe church communities that focus upon the new wine gifting of the Holy Spirit; the profound sense among many fresh expressions that the people of God rather than the building itself, is the true nature of church. Each image, stated Minear, was intended not only to describe the Church, but also to represent a normative relationship between each ecclesial grouping and the nature of the Church. The earliest Christian ecclesiology therefore employed various images that served two related purposes. They reflected characteristics the Early Church had already taken on under the leading of the Holy Spirit, and they also urged each Christian community to inhabit the images as normative for the Christian community.[18]

One of the most innovative and engaging approaches to the nature and role of the Christian Church in recent times comes from Donald Messer. Starting from one of the 'givens' of missional ecclesiology, that God's first love is the world not the Church, he offers several images of Christian mission in the form of metaphors of the Church. Church is a *covenant of global gardeners,* a metaphor garnered from the earth, because, significantly, ecological concerns are primary here. The Church must begin to reject the traditional notion of 'domination' of planet earth, and quickly abandon the spurious interpretations of Genesis that undergird it. Christians must become 'earth-keepers not earth eaters'. The Church must overcome old dualisms and learn to love the world without becoming worldly.

Church engaged in God's mission is also a *collegiality of bridge builders*: a collegiality because church is the 'reaching over' community extending grace and invitation to all, called not to create distance but to build bridges. It is a *company of star throwers*: a company because church is a fellowship of people charged with a divinely inspired and empowered mission and purpose – that of saving life. Star throwers because, in opposition to the inclination of the universe, the strong help the weak and the lost are loved, and consequently points of light twinkle amid a dark world. Church is a *community of fence movers,* those who see beyond the stale boundaries of gender, sexuality and faith or no faith – inclusiveness is the watchword. In a word, the Christian Church embodies God's *conspiracy of goodness.* This is the *missio Dei* lived out. In a world of much evil and deep injustices God has set those who conspire for goodness; they are Christian rescuers, they are authentically 'church'.[19]

- *Mission-shaped ecclesiology is inherently emerging ecclesiology*

This last element may seem superfluous, as it is assumed and to some extent demonstrated in all the other themes. Nevertheless the point is worth reiterating. The evolution of mission-shaped ecclesiology and emergence of fresh expressions is a natural consequence of the fact that God is living and dynamic rather than dead and static. The missionary nature of God, the pursuing of the *missio Dei* and the goal of the kingdom of God in a changing world naturally produce new ecclesiology and fresh expressions of church. The incarnational model of engagement that Jesus Christ exemplifies naturally involves emerging ecclesiology and new forms of church. From the beginnings of Christianity and throughout Christian history there is a continuing conversation between existing ecclesiology and emerging ecclesiology, sometimes quiet and content, sometimes heated and agitated. This is the situation today.

Without doubt a major impetus for emerging ecclesiology and fresh expressions of church today is a conviction that the complex, long-standing, religious, cultural and socio-political condition generically referred to as *Christendom* is passing away. Some mission-shaped church thinkers rightly appreciate the grandeur of much that Christendom produced and sustained, but, overall, mission-shaped ecclesiology weighs the ecclesiology of Christendom in the balance and finds it wanting. It permitted fine books to be written that dealt almost exclusively with questions of authority, and the nature of the four historical marks of the one holy catholic and apostolic Church. Christendom ecclesiology was so often written as if the Church lived in a world of its own, giving the impression of a Church turned in on itself, the sun around which all else revolves. It so often focused on its inner nature and its 'perfection' with enormous ramifications for the external identity of 'visible' church in a changing world. When it dealt with them at all, Christendom ecclesiology usually dealt with missional themes as a subset of ecclesiology rather than vice versa. Whatever else it is, therefore, mission-shaped ecclesiology is a divergence from the ecclesiology of Christendom at a number of levels. George Lings puts this poetically and powerfully:

> When you live in a house and intend staying there, questions of its decoration and furnishing seem very important and can be the cause of vigorous disagreement between the occupiers. But if you intend to sell, then what the accommodation offers, the road and area it is in, and the structural integrity of the building become far more important. In Christendom it seemed the house of the church was to be inhabited for ever so we were able to spend our time talking the ecclesiological equivalents of the furnishings and decorations.[20]

Fundamentally, then, those who believe that the essential nature and purpose of the Church is primarily missiological rather than ecclesiological, seek to reverse the Christendom maxim that the Church shapes mission. For them, the God of mission, active, alive and seeking to redeem all things, must always define and shape the Church, not vice versa. And because of that fresh expressions of church are a wonderful and welcome missiological inevitability.

To mull over . . .

- What, do you think, makes church 'church'? Do you tend naturally to 'top-down' or 'bottom-up' thinking?

- What 'marks' of the Church do you think should come alongside 'one holy catholic and apostolic'?

- Should the missionary and ecumenical movements be given 'three cheers' or 'two cheers', rather than the 'two and half cheers' they get here?

- Think of some of the images of the Church offered in the New Testament. Which images do you find the most evocative and challenging? What do you think of Donald Messer's missionary images of church outlined in this section?

- What does your own mission-shaped ecclesiology consist of?

3

Ever Emerging Church

... it is the institutional egocentricity of a
church, its unwillingness to let itself be used by
the Spirit, its wrong concept of what constitutes
'success', in short its rejection of the renewal
which is offered to it, which may cause its
sickness unto death.[1]

Visser t' Hooft

Did you see it move?
There's something there.
It's in this very cloth that I weave.
In the most peculiar ways that we behave.
It's the time of the turning and the old world's
    falling.
Nothing you can do can stop the next emerging.[2]

Peter Gabriel

Church changes

'Church changes over time,' I declared boldly to the
meeting.

'Not if our church meeting has anything to do
with it!' retorted a glum-looking man. We all know
churches like that. As the hundreds of variant 'how-
many-members-of-x-church-does-it-take-to-change-
a-light-bulb?' jokes make clear, 'change' and 'church'
are often unlikely companions in the same sentence.

In fact church does change over time and sometimes quite dramatically, but such change is not always evident, especially at the time. For example, when nobody in a church can remember a time when something was done differently, then it must always have been done like that! Mustn't it?

In my first appointment as a Methodist minister in the early 1980s, I introduced the use of a chalice into services of Holy Communion. I remember clearly being told with Yorkshire bluntness by an irate octogenarian woman that Methodism had 'always used little glasses for Communion'. Well, had it?

Individual Communion cups were patented in North America around 1894 and, as far as I can discover, arrived in the United Kingdom shortly after that. That they arrived at all was largely owing to the fact that in 1869 Thomas Welch, an American Methodist layperson, zealous teetotaller and entrepreneur, had successfully applied Louis Pasteur's processes of milk sterilization to fruit juices, producing unfermented grape juice for use at the Lord's Supper.[3] Deep (but largely mistaken) concerns about sharing dangerous microbes quickly made 'little cups' a hygienic and necessary ecclesiastical accessory in many churches of later Victorian Protestantism. Consequently, quite apart from introducing a typical form of later nineteenth-century individualism into the Christian sacrament known as 'Communion'(!), 'little glasses' can only have been in general use in British Methodism for a little over 12 decades. 'Always used little glasses'? I don't think so.

If only because many Christians slip so easily into the 'it's always been like this' mode, especially in relation to the church, a statement like 'church changes'

needs explaining and exploring. This is very important because unless it is accepted that the shape of
church can and does alter, and in line with God's will
and missionary purposes, that the apparent 'given-
ness' of inherited church – theologically, functionally
and physically – is provisional not permanent, then a
central theme of this book – that church does, will and
must continue to change radically and fundamentally
in a whole number of ways – will be resisted.

Mission historian Andrew Walls graphically
illustrates some of the massive changes occurring
through epochs in Christian history.[4] He imagines
a space time-traveller who periodically visits earth
in order to study Christianity through the groups
he encounters. In Jerusalem in 37 AD he discovers
that the original Christians are all Jews. They offer
sacrifices, circumcise their children and zealously
keep the seventh day free from work. But in 325 AD,
when he visits a gathering of Church leaders meeting at a place called Nicea there are folk from far
and near but virtually none are Jewish, indeed, if
anything, this group is anti-Jewish. Talk of sacrifice
is now talk about bread and wine used in Christian
worship. Circumcision is considered tantamount to
barbarism and the seventh day like any other day,
except the first day of the week, which is now re-
served for Christian religious observances. Unlike the
Jerusalem Christians this group seems obsessed with
the minutiae of doctrine and metaphysics. A visit to
Ireland in the sixth century dispels any impression
that all Christians are like the Nicean leaders. Monks
stand in icy water up to their necks, reciting Psalms,
arms aloft to greet the rising sun, before returning
to dark caves to eat seaweed – and all in pursuit of
personal holiness! Another visit, this time to London

in the 1840s, witnesses the launch of a mission society – 'for God, the Queen and commerce'. White men in black suits carry Bibles. Clearly doctrine is important and holiness sought, but there is little evidence that metaphysics or standing in cold water appeals to this rather well-heeled group. A further visit, to Nigeria in the 1980s, presents yet another picture. Christianity now seems dominated by black people in white robes, singing songs and inviting people to their church to experience the supernatural power of a holy God.

Just as it takes an occasional visitor to our homes to see what we do not see, to note changes – how the children have grown, who has lost hair or gained weight – so viewing Christianity through historical paradigms makes clear the extent of change. Christianity changes over time, and closely interconnected to all such changes in Christianity is the emergence of fresh expressions of church. How could it be otherwise?

The church of earliest Christianity emerged and developed out of the Temple in Jerusalem, the synagogues of scattered Judaism, and the profound role of the home in Jewish life. Christians (though, of course, they were not yet called by that name) in Jerusalem worshipped in the Temple with all that that entailed.[5] But it is clear from the outset that 'Temple church' was supplemented with 'home church' which probably included acts of worship in the open air in both private and public settings. Gathering in homes for 'victuals and rituals' was not novel but was a regular part of Jewish life, and Jews who became 'believers' continued to gather together in this way, the group of believers effectively constituting 'the family' or 'the household'.[6]

Following the death of Stephen (Acts 7) and the beginnings of persecution Christian believers scattered from Jerusalem, and the synagogues in cities and towns throughout the Roman Empire, often founded by Jews of earlier 'scatterings', became 'church' for many of them. It was in the synagogues, located not in the rarefied air of Jerusalem but in the pluralist atmosphere of the Greco-Roman world, that Christian believers established themselves and shared their faith with God-fearers and proselytes, with non-Jews. This transmission of faith resulted in different things happening in different places at different speeds. In some synagogues Jews and Christians apparently coexisted quite amicably for quite a time. Some synagogues were taken over and effectively became Christian 'churches'. In many instances, realizing what was happening, the Jewish synagogue elders expelled believers, both Jew and Gentile, who went on to form their own 'church', in homes rather than specially constructed buildings, taking some aspects of synagogue life and worship with them[7] but essentially providing the possibility of distinctly Christian worship and fellowship for the first time.

'Church' in the 'households' of Christian believers in the Greco-Roman world was as formative and influential as the home churches of the earliest Jewish believers.[8] Indeed, communities formed by both Jewish and Gentile Christians in their homes provide the most common model of 'church' in early Jewish and Gentile Christianity. This is not to suggest that these communities were all alike, or that by 'home church' we should think of a contemporary group sitting on couches, chatting and drinking coffee. Abraham Malherbe points out that a 'household' in the Early Church era was a 'basic political unit' consisting not only of members of the immediate family but also a combination of slaves, freed people, servants and labourers, tenants and even business partners or associates. Such a household engendered deep loyalty to the interests of the household among its members. It provided a sense of belonging, closeness, security and solidarity that went beyond economics to include psychological, social and religious factors.[9] It was factors such as these that enabled the Church to survive and even to grow slightly amidst times of social ostracism and active persecution in the first three centuries. 'Household churches' then, represent a larger, more socially complex community than is normally suggested by the term 'home church' meeting in the dwelling of a nuclear family. J.G. Davies pointed out that in some places 'before the fourth century . . . Christians were in the habit of meeting for worship no longer in private houses but in large buildings especially constructed for the purpose'.[10] Nevertheless, overall, Early Church worship often possessed the intimate characteristics of gatherings for family prayers – albeit the prayers of a large family. The role and value of home churches in the Jewish and early Hellenist eras of Christianity is hard to overestimate.

If this all sounds rather grand we must also remember that other, more humble – but very moving – family church images arise out of early Christianity. Celsus, a critic and enemy of the Church, ridicules Christianity for its *social inclusion*, especially of lower social classes and women. 'In private houses also we see wool-workers, cobblers, laundry-workers, and the most illiterate and bucolic yokels . . .' Christians urge such people to 'go along with the women and the little children . . . to the wooldresser's shop . . . that they may learn perfection. And by saying this they persuade them.'[11] The *generosity and hospitality* of early Christianity was also clearly a prominent characteristic.[12] Alan Kreider draws attention to a winsome characteristic of Early Church life he calls 'witness through mercy'. Clearly, and in spite of unpopularity and sometimes danger the Church was never turned in on itself. In an attempt to reinstate paganism as the official religion of the Roman Empire, and oust Christianity from that newly found position, the ex-Christian Emperor Julian gives a revealing example of this. ' . . . it is their benevolence to strangers, their care for the graves of the dead and the pretend holiness of their lives that have done most to increase their atheism . . . the impious Galileans support not only their own poor but ours as well.'[13] Yet not long before this period, there existed what Robert Warren calls 'the *church-of-the-catacombs*. Here the church met underground in the vast burial places in Rome which eventually covered twenty kilometres of underground passages in which half a million Christians were buried.'[14] Nor, finally, was Early Church life as *tame* as church in homes might signal. In a marvellous blast at the Church the pagan Caecilius stated Christians 'are a gang of discredited and prescribed desperadoes . . . They have gathered together from the lowest dregs of the populace ignorant men and credulous women . . . and have formed a rabble of impious conspirators . . . they fall in love almost before they are acquainted; everywhere they introduce a kind of religious lust . . .'[15] My own suggestion is that if you find a church like that – join it!

The point is clear I think. The Early Church was far from monochrome or homogeneous. It was full of variety, of emerging and fresh expressions of Christian communities.

By the earlier Middle Ages dedicated 'church build-ings' (as opposed to adapted buildings) had arrived in earnest. There were two dominant expressions of church: the basilicas and cathedrals situated mainly in the cities and towns of Christendom, and monas-teries and abbeys often (at first) located away from centres of population. Both came in a bewildering variety of types and sizes, though there were domin-ant designs. It is interesting to note that, broadly speaking, basilicas were an expression of church that *engaged* culture and society whereas monasteries, at least in the early period, arose from attempts to *disengage* from the prevailing culture and society. Both basilica and monastery were missionary in different ways. The basilica was primarily an ex-pression of an incultured Christianity at home in the society of its day, the monastery primarily an expression of a pilgrim Christianity seeking to em-plant and embody a new society within the old. The basilica model of church took on the shape and space of power and privilege, as no doubt was thought to befit a religion now authorized by the Holy Roman Empire. The basilicas and cathedrals were, after all, church modelled on the law courts, and bishops came to sit in session in much the same way that lawyers did. So whereas the main expression of church in the early centuries was largely contextually *domestic*, by the time Christianity was the official religion of the Holy Roman Empire the main expression of church was largely contextually *public and legal-istic*. Here again there was a 'minority schedule', another way of being church. This came through certain monastic communities and especially through Celtic Christianity and its tantalizing glimpses of *people-group churches*, Christian communities very different from the Roman parish system that replaced it.[16]

From the later Middle Ages, right through the Reformation period and the Enlightenment era the single most dominant shape of church was provided by the parishes systems of 'established' churches'.[17] If a country was 'Christian' then its territories were covered by a matrix of church buildings and governance that made clear this fact. Although not 'established' in a formal sense, both the denominations of nonconformity and the new congregations of renewalist Christianity are variants of this shape of church.

But within this macro picture, as we have seen from examples of Early Church life, there is change and development occurring at national and regional levels and in response to more localized factors. In Britain, for example, the Methodist movement of the later eighteenth century produced its own fresh expressions of class meetings and societies, adapting a social model of 'clubs' and 'associations' that were emerging in wider society at the time. It is worth noting that each new form of church reflects a move to renewed discipleship that provides structures enabling both intimacy and authenticity alongside a missionary evangelistic impulse. In other words the inner resources of church are matched by outward urges.

Why does church change?

A short response to this question is (a) because God wants it to, in order to share in the *missio Dei*, (b) because the Christian Church is incarnational by nature, like Jesus Christ its Lord and (c) because it is impelled to change by the Holy Spirit of God who is a Spirit of mission. However, perhaps a little more unpacking is required.

The ability of Christianity – and its churches – to change in relation to its cultural context is a great blessing and one made clear in the history of mission. Without the ability to cross cultural boundaries Christianity would never have survived the Jewish-Roman war of the first century, still less the demise of the (Christianized) Roman Empire. There would have never been a Gentile converted to the faith, still less a Slav, a Celt or an Inuit. Christianity would have withered on its first vine, rendering reproduction impossible. 'Translatability' – as Lamin Sanneh calls it[18] – is one of the great geniuses of Christianity. That Christianity can take root in different soils and produce true Christian disciples around the world, down the centuries and up into heaven is nothing short of miraculous. That there are Christians around the world today is living testimony to the metamorphic qualities of the Christian faith. Without suggesting that every fresh expression of church that has ever occurred lies fully in the will and purpose of God (which is an unsustainable assertion), it is a statement of fact that church understood as a vessel and agent of God's redemptive mission in the world changes as an inevitable consequence of fulfilling its calling.

Given the nature of the Christian faith, why should we be surprised at this? Taking its lead from its divine Lord an incarnational religion like Christianity is always going to be changing shape in order that the gospel can be authentically offered to each new generation, to each new cultural context, to each emerging social environment. If Christianity were unchanging, if it could not incarnate and communicate God's gospel news to each and every changing context, then how could it truly be the expression of Christ at all? George Lings suggests that the doctrines of the incarnation and resurrection are profoundly significant for contemporary ecclesiology, and especially in relation to fresh expressions, because they model both continuity and change. The incarnation and resurrection of Jesus Christ makes clear that change can happen without destroying identity.

The prime agent of mission is God the Holy Spirit. My own Methodist tradition has a rich view of the Holy Spirit. John Wesley spoke about and relied upon the Holy Spirit in terms of what he called prevenient grace. Put simply, this marvellous theme acknowledged God's 'going beforeness' into every context and situation. When Christians declared their faith to unbelievers, when missionaries entered uncharted territories, when witness to Jesus took place in contexts seemingly impervious to the gospel, of one thing Christians could be sure: God the Holy Spirit had 'gone before', preparing a way, already there, in the world. Even before believers could get comfortable in Jerusalem and start settling down, the Spirit impelled them out from that place 'to the ends of the earth'.

In recent times the Holy Spirit has probably been portrayed more in 'charismatic' than missional terms. Hundreds of seminars and books have taught about charismatic gifts, and particularly the gift of tongues. The Spirit's role has been mainly conceived as 'bringing gifts to the church' and 'building up the body of Christ', and as a non-demonstrative charismatic (!) I rejoice in the life Spirit Renewal has brought to contemporary Christianity. But I do sometimes wonder if our concept of renewal is not sometimes a bit inward looking, if we have not tried to domesticate the Spirit of God as a 'pet' of the Church, if the focus on the Spirit as Renewer of the Church has inadvertently taken our gaze off other, even more primary biblical Spirit themes – like mission. The Acts of the Apostles (some say it should be called the 'Acts of the Holy Spirit') make it clear that the primary work of the Spirit is missionary and evangelistic. In other words, the Holy Spirit in Acts is less like the oil of chrism and more like WD40 – freeing up rather than blessing up! On the Day of Pentecost it is clear that Luke considers the most significant thing about this charismatic happening and arrival of tongues is not the ecstasy of the believers (wonderful though it was). Nor is it the 'building up of the Church' (though no doubt the whole occasion was a marvellous encouragement). *The* most important thing is missional. It is that people from all over the world understood the believers; that they heard the praises of God and the gospel of Christ declared to them in their own tongue. Those who needed to hear the gospel did, declaring, in effect 'they're speaking my language'. The Holy Spirit's main role in Acts is to empower the Church to mission and evangelism, to bless it in order that it is a blessing, rather than blessed for its own sake.[19]

But as well as a blessing, this 'translatability' of church poses hard questions. What, it might be asked, is Christianity? What holds it all together? Is there a 'real' Christianity at all or is it merely a chameleon faith? Has it a 'core' or does it just shape itself around whichever cultural context it happens to be in? I respond to such challenging questions by noting that in every historical expression of Christianity there are strands of continuity amid considerable discontinuity. Whether in the homes of the Early Church, the basilicas and cathedrals of Christendom, the monasteries of the Middle Ages, the parishes of establishment, the denominations of nonconformity or the new congregations of renewal there are common threads. For example, there is always a community, always worship, a credo to live by, the use of Scriptures, beliefs – in Jesus Christ as Saviour and Lord – and so on.

However, we must be clear about the nature of this continuity. In any particular historical context there will be the use of Scripture, but *how* Scripture is used may alter from era to era. In every historical era the Church will profess belief in Jesus Christ, but the dominant beliefs about him will change from era to era. The continuity is a continuity of themes and values more than of unaltered content or expression. This notion of continuity and its nature is important if only because the popularity of paradigm shift theories, culled from sciences and sometimes awkwardly applied to non-science contexts such as theology and Christian history, tend to overemphasize discontinuity. The changes of Christianity are considerable but there is continuity. A tractor does not become a camel but a pupa does become a butterfly.

Church too has continuity amid discontinuity. Again the continuity is more about values and themes than expressions. The expressions can be many and varied but there will always be community, worship, ritual, credo, Scripture and structure. In a time when we are witnessing the accelerating demise of 'inherited church' – the territorial 'building' model of late Christendom – and the arrival of multiple fresh expressions of church, this sort of continuity will light our way. If 'fresh' means having-values-and-themes-unlike-any-other-ecclesial-grouping-ever then we must be very wary indeed. 'Fresh expressions' are just that – new expressions of the continuity of themes and values of the Christian Church in a new context, rather than discontinuous with them at a profound level. So, if one strand of ecclesial continuity is that a community of Christ's disciples gathers around certain beliefs and rituals, then, even if the congregations, the congregants and the nature of the gathering and scattering differ greatly from previous expressions, 'church' is expressed.

There are, of course, perennial debates about whether the changes the Church undergoes are the right changes. In a previous book I outlined the relationship of Christianity to its broad cultural context[20] and argued that this was a complex and challenging balancing act. Put simply the Christian Church has to walk the line between simple capitulation to a prevailing culture, melting into it and losing its identity as God's prophetic sign to the world, while on the other hand resisting the temptation to withdraw from the world in glorious isolation, which denies the essential missionary nature of the Church. In short, in relation to its cultural context the Church cannot opt out, but mustn't fall in. In each great period of Christian history, as we have seen, there have usually been expressions of church that tend to the incultured, engaged mode, and ecclesial expressions which call people out from 'the world' to form church. This is no accident, and we should expect various fresh expressions of both 'engaged' and 'called out' church to emerge in our own changing cultural context as a natural consequence of the Church finding its primary identity and character in the *missio Dei*.

Mixed economies: challenge, cost and constituencies

Christianity, then, changes – as do expressions of church as an intrinsic part of that process. Fresh expressions of church are not new – new forms of church have accompanied every era of Christian mission and witness since the day of Pentecost. What we describe today as fresh expressions, emerging church, new ways of being church and the like, is normative for a faith like Christianity. It's wonderful, but entirely normal. Fresh expressions are also signs of two different realities. First is the comforting reality that the missionary Spirit of God has not given up on us, that we in the Church today continue to be called to share in God's mission. Second is the challenging reality that, precisely in order to share in God's mission, a greater variety of expressions of church are required than the recent past provides.

One reason why the present time is so exciting is the sheer *variety* of fresh expressions emerging. This itself is significant as for a long time in the West a certain model and understanding of church has been so dominant as to monopolize the term 'church'; what Robert Warren calls 'inherited church' and defines as 'church = building + priest + stipend'.[21] The days of monolithic monopoly church models are passing away, however. In both our wider society and the life of the Christian Church we are clearly in a crucial time of 'inbetweenness' or (as some more erudite writers put it) 'liminality'. Western Christians are living through a time of enormous cultural transition: from modern to postmodern, Christian to post-Christian, Christendom to post-Christendom. Such a context requires a variety of expressions of church in order that the Church is a useful partner in the *missio Dei*.

We are wise, therefore, to attend to *both* 'inherited' church and 'emerging' church, producing what Rowan Williams refers to as a 'mixed economy'. For a while yet inherited church, provided it does well the 'basics' of witness, worship and pastoral care (and sadly not all do), will continue to be effectively missional in a variety of environments and contexts. Consequently, the move to fresh expressions must not be and cannot be a complete, speedy abandonment of inherited church. We remain in a both-and rather than an either-or situation. Alongside inherited church, however, is the burgeoning of new ways of being church that are no longer quirky exceptions to the inherited norm but increasingly a norm itself. Church plants, base communities, multiple congregations, cell church models, home church models, workplace churches, and fresh expressions we have not yet seen, need to be recognized among us for what they are – expressions of 'proper' church. Energy is a useful analogy. The production of energy was once simply talk about coal and gas. Now the debate – contentious and passionate – locates itself also around wind power, nuclear power and recently 'micro generation', where each farm or even each home will produce as well as consume energy. Old energy moves towards exhaustion and an increasingly mixed economy will continue to emerge in the future.

A key element in the strategy of a mixed economy of church, and one that affects all Christian groupings but especially older denominations like my own, concerns the issue of allocating resources. This not only (certainly) involves money but also (the best) personnel, creative time and energy. This is the acid test for many who have belonged and contributed to inherited church all their lives, and at some cost. Our existing inherited churches, those ageing 'fresh expressions' of the past seem always to demand the lion's share of whatever there is! The routes for allocating money to prop up multiple failing causes (in order to 'sustain the mission'!) are well entrenched. The production of clergy who 'service' the status quo is well established. The pattern and demands of belonging to inherited church is well defined. The inherited system of 'doing church' is spoken for and leaves little time or energy left over for new ventures or versions. Experts in congregational studies suggest that any new ministry taken on by a local church will require large proportions of disposable money, time and personnel to be allocated to it for several years, before it can truly be said that it has been *tried* with any seriousness.[22] All this means that strong resolve is needed to shift more – and more appropriate – resources into emerging church. The speed at which varieties of fresh expressions of church emerge is clearly dependent in part upon whether the custodians of inherited church resources hold fast to them or release them. The mixed economy, then, will best be undertaken by historic denominations through strategic and intentional management, rather than incidentally and accidentally, and, whenever possible, regionally and nationally as well as locally. Fresh expressions are not produced simply by top-down decisions, but they are significantly encouraged and enabled when denominational authorities work with rather than against the will of the Holy Spirit.

Consequently, one of the sure signs that God is 'in' this fresh expressions thing is that many inherited church people are becoming increasingly convicted and convinced that shifting the balance of resources towards new ways of being church is right under God. In my experience this is certainly true of considerable numbers of my parents' and parents-in-law's generation, with a lifetime of belonging to inherited church. They do not need to be personally involved in fresh expressions – though some are – to support the view that much prayerful and practical support is required, and they often take a vicarious joy and pride in the fact that 'something new is happening'. The full impact of resourcing fresh expressions upon inherited church life, in terms of sustaining its own life and ministry has not yet been profoundly felt, and a (piecemeal) 'both-and' approach has been possible to date in many instances. A starker 'either-or' choice between sustaining inherited church or resourcing fresh expressions, which will arise increasingly in the near future, may result in a different response from this generation of church members, but my inclination is to suggest that this generation is often more open than its ministers to changing direction, even at some cost to its own patterns of discipleship.

I have often preached from the gospel passage where Jesus says 'Those who want to save their life will lose it, and those who lose their life for my sake will find it.'[23] Usually I have applied it to individuals: '*You* will find your life by giving it to Christ.' In recent years, however, I have also begun to apply this gospel principle to congregations. 'Hold on to your life together and you will lose it. Give it away for the sake of the Saviour, and enlist again in his missionary evangelistic service, and you will find it.' Such relinquishing of proprietorial ownership over 'your' local church is a profound gospel challenge.

Also, such a conversion does not necessarily guarantee 'success' – whatever we might mean by that – but it does guarantee that a congregation becomes more profoundly mission-shaped and mission-minded and thereby more truly church. Costly though this challenge is, I am increasingly encouraged and thrilled by the numbers of inherited church congregations that begin to take it up, so much so that I have begun to reflect why this is so.

To be sure, some of the openness to change in inherited church is born of desperation. Change is accepted when there is no other option, like deciding to leave the house and get in the boat as the water reaches your neck as you stand in the upstairs bedroom! Equally, some readiness to change is born of exhaustion; so many loyal Christians in inherited church are simply weary with it all. A proper pastoral role today, therefore, is telling good and faithful servants who have, over many decades, innocently but surely mistaken Christian discipleship for keeping the local church solvent, that they can now lay down that role with dignity and be released from its burden. Still another reason – perhaps more prevalent than we might admit among ourselves – is that many are not just weary, but are sick and tired of inherited church and were it not for a deep sense of loyalty would pack it in tomorrow. It is absolutely vital, however, that alongside this 'laying down' and 'releasing', the mission of God, and the call of God to the Church to participate in it, and the invitation of God to people like us to share in it, is rehearsed and proclaimed. Through this, new opportunities for discipleship will be explored and encouraged. My friends in their forties and fifties, long-term church members, need to hear *both* these messages for the sake of their spirits.

But also, crucially, readiness to change among inherited church members is also arising from the flickerings of renewed vision. Through the wooing of the missionary Spirit the message of mission-shaped church strikes a chord, like a song long forgotten but faintly familiar, and when a congregation begins to sing the new song they know instinctively that they are becoming more fully what God created and desires them to be. They understand anew that they are a death and resurrection people, and being mission-shaped is in their blood. They realize afresh that Jesus said *he* would build his Church and told his followers to make disciples – and not vice versa – and in resolving to obey their Lord's command a new energy, vitality and faith-confidence surprises them with joy. Inherited church people begin to regard fresh expressions as forms of mission and ministry engaging people untouched by their own church life. Rather than a threat or 'competition', they begin to look upon fresh expressions as potential spiritual homes for those people. Such people probably include members of their own families and friends and neighbours, while others will be the 'fruit' of their own ministry and mission over the years, but for whom an inherited church environment has proved increasingly impossible. And all this becomes a cause for rejoicing! More than that the impulse to develop fresh expression in their own local church takes root. This has certainly been the case for some of my friends in their thirties and forties. Almost finished with inherited church and out of the door they wonderfully, with relatively little encouragement, grasp the vision that God is not yet finished with them or the Church. They begin to find a new vitality in discipleship through exploring a new form of church. Fresh expressions, you see, do not merely replace inherited churches they also emerge out of them.

Making the case

Over the course of the previous chapters a case for fresh expressions has been building up, and before moving on to other topics I rehearse some of the main themes here.

- *Fresh expressions incarnate quite naturally key aspects of Christian faith and values.*

  Fresh expressions embody powerfully several important theological motifs – birth, life, risk, hope, fragility and engagement, to mention just a few. Such motifs are not *all* the gospel but they *are* all gospel motifs and emphasize valuable and core themes without which Christian witness and life are poorer and out of balance. While aware of the danger of stereotyping, it is the case that such gospel themes as these seem to arise naturally out of fresh expressions in a way that is not always evident in the life of inherited churches.

- *Fresh expressions can be models for the renewal of the Church in the mission of God.*

  In particular, fresh expressions are often able to model the mission of God outlined earlier. In fresh expressions we often see, more powerfully and regularly than in many inherited churches, a move beyond a nodded theological assent or lip-service to God's mission. Fresh expressions, perhaps with the advantage of beginning something afresh, often become church communities whose lives and lips agree about the defining nature of this doctrine in terms of it shaping their lives. This is not to say that recent fresh expressions have a monopoly on being 'mission-shaped churches'; they do not. Fresh expressions do, however, model church in a variety of forms and shapes, in a way that expresses God's mission – and they are an important exemplar to the whole Church.

- *Rather than a churchy way of thinking, fresh expressions embody a kingdom-of-God mindset.*

Fresh expressions also model the aim and goal of the *missio Dei* outlined earlier, namely the coming of the kingdom – or reign – of God. They adopt a natural mission-shaped ecclesiology and embody the conviction that missiology shapes ecclesiology, and not vice versa. The effects of this, in a variety of subtle ways, are a sense that the Church is for God and the world and only then, in any sense, for itself. This contrasts sharply with the impression given (deliberately or not) by many inherited churches, especially those in decline, or wrestling with the costs of keeping huge buildings running or appealing for large sums to sustain historic ministries, that the main aim of church is keeping the show on the road, maintaining a status quo, focusing inwards rather than outwards.

- *Rejecting fresh expressions is like denying how we got to be here at all.*

Churches in every age, place and time, whether 10, 100, or 1,000 years ago, were once freshly planted. The nature of fresh expressions has undoubtedly altered throughout Christian history, being shaped by many factors and forces, but fundamentally all church began as fresh expressions. Consequently, for a cell, group, congregation or denomination to reject fresh expressions or to respond in a way that lessens the possibility of their springing up, by lack of resources or theological intention, is to commit slow suicide.

- *Fresh expressions are built upon that most profound Christian motif: death and resurrection.*

Donald English used to speak of death and resurrection as the way God designs not only the gospel story, but everything God has created. If so, that includes the Church: church, in all its forms goes through death and resurrection, just as its Lord did. Fresh expressions are the key means of incarnating ecclesial resurrection and, by implication, death.

- *Fresh expressions are a potentially invaluable method of Christian witness and evangelism in our contemporary pluralist, multifaith cultural context.*

Inherited church has the advantage, in this, the twilight of Christendom, of still being recognized as 'church'. But this advantage is also a disadvantage. Being recognized as 'church' today means that such a church represents and embodies Christian history and a Christendom outlook. Warts and all, as, for many people today, of all faiths and none, it is the abuse of power and the horror stories of history that come most quickly to mind. As a result, inherited church is quickly regarded as tarnished in terms of its ability to incarnate authentic, humble, often very local, Christianity. Fresh expressions are, of course, not technically absolved from their place in the great tradition of the Church, but the fact that they often do not fulfil the stereotype of inherited Church enables them to operate differently, offer a different model of being Christian and being church. In these days where religious sensitivities run high, fresh expressions that are able to look different and feel different to that which is normally accepted and encountered as 'church' are able to communicate Christianity differently to non-Christians and other faith groups alike. Certainly this appears to be true among my lovely but essentially nominally Christian friends. 'Church' is spoken for and they do not think much of what it speaks. I remember taking a good friend to a student café church one morning and he loved it: the friendliness, lack of pretension and clear love and devotion of the worshippers all made a lasting and positive impression.

- *Fresh expressions, then, express different models of ecclesia to inherited church, some of which are especially significant in relation to our constantly changing cultural context.*

Fresh expressions, as part of the 'mixed economy', offer valuable means of doing several important things differently. They enable new and different people to become Christian disciples. They seem to enable a different kind of belonging, commitment and participation among lay people to the 'passive receptor' model of many inherited churches. They require, and therefore generate, different kinds of leadership from that often produced for inherited churches. Their 'internal life' tends to be configured around a different group of meetings and different models of relationality than many inherited churches.

- *Lastly fresh expressions tend to produce fresh expressions and therefore remind us that church is, God intentionally, fertile and reproductive*

Fresh expressions are thus signs of hope and signals of better ways of being church as we enter the challenge and opportunity of the emerging future.

To mull over . . .

- What is important to you in your church that you recognize was once an innovation? What was the previous way of doing things?

- If you were to start your church tomorrow with the same people, what would it look like?

- What three things in the life of your church are most important to you? What three things (or more!) would you happily stop doing?

- What, for you, might be attractive about being part of a fresh expression? What might be fearful?

- What is the Spirit saying to you and your church? How do you discern this? What are you doing about it?

4

Shapers of Future Church

If Christianity cannot be inculturated
successfully within the postmodern context,
there will be no Western Church.[1]

Graham Cray

People cry out to God when the ground under
their feet is shaking – only to discover it is God
who is shaking it.

Anon

This chapter is an attempt to outline what I believe to
be three of the key 'shapers' of inherited churches and
fresh expressions alike. Taken together these related
themes have had a profound effect on the shaping of
contemporary church – inherited, transitional and
emerging – and I believe they will continue to do so
in the immediate future.

Culture shapers

Each of these 'shapers' is in some respect a positive
and negative response to a broad western cultural
context that has witnessed the long-term decline
of power, popularity and prestige of the Christian
Church. Books attempting to map out the contours
of this bewildering cultural context account for more

felled trees than most topics nowadays, and there is no need for any lengthy attempt at cultural analysis here.[2] Yet the scene needs to be set, if only in bald outline, because our cultural context is the stage on which the life of contemporary corporate Christianity is lived out. One way of interpreting our broad cultural landscape is in terms of 'posts' which together mark out the land on which western Christianity currently lives, breathes and has its (earthly) being.

Postmodernity

The first 'post' is *postmodernity*, a catch-all term basically expressing awareness that things are not what they used to be in almost any respect. Sometimes written 'post-modernity' it is a collection of cultural, aesthetic, political and philosophical observations that attempt to describe, define and assess the shift from the 'modern' era to the postmodern era. So, for example, the (supposed) mono-cultural nature of modernity has become the plurality of postmodernity, in which contradictory truth-claims result in the inevitable rejection that truth can be absolute or found in one place – like in a single religious system. Consequently theories that account for 'life, the universe and everything' – like Christianity – are increasingly rejected as incredible and replaced with personal convictions, stories and opinions. Fundamentally postmodernity puts big question marks next to many of the major themes of modernity (such as a belief that rationality leads inevitably to progress and betterment) and declares them 'not enough'. I imagine many Christians will resonate with that. Postmodern people tend to construct their own meanings by which they live. They are regarded as consumers rather than producers, and find identity in leisure and interests rather than occupations and employment. They tend to live for today rather than yesterday or tomorrow. They tend to be 'life' orientated rather than 'death' orientated (with all sorts of ramifications for how a faith like Christianity is encountered). They belong to a credit card society rather than a savings card society. For our purposes here it is sufficient to note that a recurrent theme in mission-shaped church thinking is the (sometimes too easily made) assumption that 'inherited church' is essentially but understandably an ecclesial expression of the shapes, structures and mindsets of modernity, whereas emerging church embodies, in different ways and to different degrees the messy marks and traits of postmodernity.

The two remaining 'posts' derive from post-modernity in the sense that they are responses to it and focus more particularly upon Christianity in the light of it.

Post-Christendom

The second 'post' is *post-Christendom* and is of particular interest to missiologists and those reflecting on the shape of Christian life and faith in the present time. Put simply, post-Christendom is the term used to assert that Christianity is emerging from a cultural religious era known as Christendom. Of course the term 'Christendom' has long been used in histories of Christianity to identify an era in which Christ's kingdom was the dominant shaper of culture and society – the kingdom come on earth (sort of) as it is in heaven. In particular it signals the adoption of Christianity as the official religion of a city or state or empire, with the result that a 'Christian culture' comes about. As a consequence Christian beliefs, rituals, practices and morality become normative, as they are defined, pronounced and enforced by leaders of the state, both 'sacred' and 'secular' who are, by definition, 'Christian'. In a basic sense therefore, *post*-Christendom simply means a time after this Christendom era has ended. In most mission-shaped writing today post-Christendom means just that and more, becoming a generic term for any aspect of the life of the contemporary church that is seen to *have* left Christendom behind, or, any remaining aspect of Christendom that it is deemed to *need* to leave behind.

Stuart Murray offers the following working definition: 'Post-Christendom is the culture that emerges as the Christian faith loses coherence within a society that has been definitively shaped by the Christian story and as the institutions that have been developed to express Christian convictions decline in influence.'[3] In expanding this statement he talks of a series of transitions from Christendom that give shape to post-Christendom. There is a shift from the centre of society to its margins, from a situation where Christianity, instead of being the majority, is a minority, from a settled 'at home-ness' in Christendom to a more sojourning pilgrim mode in post-Christendom. There is a shift from a context of privilege to one of plurality, from a situation of considerable control to one where influence comes mainly through witness and distinctive lifestyle. There is a shift from maintenance to mission. (This common one-liner of mission-shaped thinking has some Christian leaders incandescent, stating with some justification that these are not mutually exclusive. In terms of the transition to post-Christendom, however, 'maintenance to mission' signals a significant evolution of a culture maintaining a supposed Christian status quo

and one recognizing it is in an increasingly challenging missionary environment.) There is the shift
from Church understood essentially as an institution
to church as a movement.[4] The fourth century witnessed what is sometimes termed the 'Constantinian
Reversal', when the Roman Emperor Constantine
adopted Christianity as the favoured state religion
and thereby 'reversed' the time when Christianity
was effectively outlawed. Today we are witnessing
the reversal of Constantinianism, an end to an era of
Christianity as a state-adopted religion.

In addition to looking backwards – which is what
'post' words essentially do – the term post-Christendom is also used to outline emerging phenomena and
traits of the Christian Church. Just what it *means* for
the Christian Church to be a marginalized minority,
in a plural, missionary context; just what is *involved*
for Christians today, as sojourners and witnesses belonging to a missionary movement, is a crucial theme
in mission-shaped church thinking, and therefore a
key tributary to the themes of this book.

Post-Christianity

The third 'post' is *post-Christianity*. This is the
recognition that contemporary western culture, so
profoundly shaped by Christianity in all manner of
ways in times past, is increasingly past all that. The
doctrines and structures of the Christian religion
impact and shape our lives and societies decreasingly
today. 'The missing God who is not missed'[5] as one
writer puts it. Post-Christianity is evident in the work
of some theologians and is a core subject of sociologists of religion. Steve Bruce, for example, remains a
staunch supporter of the inexorable secularization of
the West, and rejects the thinking of any social scien-

tists and Church leaders who try to minimize its effect by talk of pervasive religiosity and Christian belief in spite of sharply declining churchgoing.[6] Put simply, he does not provide much encouragement for optimism in Christian folk, in respect of either inherited *or* fresh expressions of church. Other sociologists such as Grace Davie and Robin Gill offer models of secularization no less challenging than Bruce's, but which, at least theoretically, leave open more possibilities for the revitalization of Christianity in the West.[7] None of them suggests an easy future.

Clive Marsh writes about a 'post-atheist' rather than a post-Christian age and articulates his own convictions about the patterns of belief and belonging required as Christianity enters the immediate future. He regards our present cultural climate 'as an age within which religion (or, at least, religiosity and spirituality) might again find a place. At a time when the reach of an all-consuming technocratic rationality is questioned, religion can again find its place amongst the channels through which mystery, humanness, limitation, and awe reassert themselves.'[8] Standing in the liberal Protestant tradition, Marsh's prescriptions both chime with and challenge evangelical and charismatic agendas about the future of church in Britain, strengthening my own conviction that both historic liberalism and evangelicalism alike were profoundly shaped by modernity and are now in the process of being reconfigured for life in our post-Christian environment.

Predictions about religion in the West in general, then, and traditional and emerging forms of Christianity as a still significant part of the scene, remain varied. Some scholars prophesy further decline and imminent meltdown. Others suggest transformation rather than terminal illness. However, most of the transformation scenarios hold little good news for inherited church and its mode of being, and not much more hope for fresh expressions either, predicting as they do a shift from theism to pantheism, from God to 'self-as-god' and from formal religion to (implicit) spirituality.[9] It is in wider contexts such as this that mission-shaped church thinking takes place and inherited, fresh and emerging expressions of church live out their lives.

A little good news?

Amid all the bad news banner headlines about the inevitable decline and imminent demise of the Church in Britain there is, I believe, some 'good news' and grounds for proper hope for the future of the Christian Church in the West. Without minimizing the challenge of our broad cultural context outlined above, or the depressing trends of recent decades, the good news amounts to more than clutching at straws in a high wind.

- *The first piece of good news is that there is little good news at all, from almost any source whatsoever, for poor models of traditional inherited church!*

So whenever the basics of being church – mission and evangelism, worship, pastoral care, leadership, fellowship, sacred space and so on – are poor, there would seem to be an ever bleaker future for that model of church. Human beings are not populating such poor expressions of church (some would say even 'non-church') and, although God has not withdrawn from it, seems not be putting many eggs in that particular basket. This is the first piece of good news! Good news in the sense that sustaining poor church does not work and will not work. Good news in the sense that lovely, faithful, loyal church folk in such congregations can and must be released from the moving mentality that sustaining such poor church is their Christian duty. We can move on. Christian discipleship does not involve keeping poor church in business.

A second piece of good news needs to be held closely together to the first, in order to prevent unnecessary despair. It is this.

- *Whenever the 'basics' of being church are revisited and new mission-shaped focus implemented, whenever 'good' church begins to emerge out of 'poor', the result is almost always a revitalization of the existing congregation and sometimes a growth of the existing congregation.*

- In a nutshell, there is little human hope for poor inherited churches, but there is cause for some hope for inherited church in transition, church that begins to get its act together – with the leading and infilling of the missionary Spirit of God. Some of the material that follows, then, is not so much about 'emerging church' as about how inherited churches might engage in transition to become better churches in their own right.

The third piece of good news is already implicit in this book.

- *Alongside inherited church decline, and inherited churches undergoing transition, are emerging fresh expressions of church of various kinds.*

Related to clues about how churches transition to greater mission-shapedness, but essentially distinct from inherited churches in several respects, these signal a wider mixed economy that we might yet dare to hope for. Some of the material that follows relates more to these than inherited church. All of these bring hope.

The one thing necessary . . .

Before proceeding, there is one indispensable factor, without which there is no real hope at all, whether for inherited church in transition or the most innovative fresh expression. Prayerful openness to the Spirit of the missionary God is a crucial, necessary starting point. Whenever a local church realizes that things are not as they should be, nor as God wants them to be, and begins to explore the 'so whats' that flow from this sense of divine discontent, the first vital step is taken towards potential renewal. It is not 'change for change's sake'. It is not that any old change will do. Changing the water in the flower vases is necessary but of itself will probably not do it. Local churches that move intentionally (and often painfully) to develop a mentality of openness to change, of strategic change, of change they believe to be Spirit-led, even at great cost to their inherited ways and local traditions, start to become a more healthy mission shape. Similarly those called to engage in fresh expressions and emerging churches of bewildering variety and colour require the leading and discernment of the missionary Spirit of God no less. The last piece of good news is this. When God's people seek to become mission-shaped church, modestly or radically, when they open up to the possibility of painful renewal, they can be certain of one thing: the presence and the leading of God.

To mull over . . .

- Which traits of 'postmodern people' outlined here ring most true in your own experience?

- To what extent do you think you are living in a post-Christendom situation today? In what ways does your church respond to this situation?

- What term best describes the people living in your local neighbourhood, post-Christian or post-atheist? Why?

- How good is the good news outlined in this chapter?

- To what degree are you – and your church – experiencing 'divine discontent'? What might be your response to it?

5

Challenging Clues and Hope-filled Hints – Inherited Churches in Transition

The church begins to die whenever the religious practice of Christians is disengaged from the world in which they live.[1]

Paul Chilcote

Where the church is on a downward spiral, continuing to do what it already does is not an answer . . . only change offers the possibility of reversing the slide.[2]

Maggie Durran

In recent times some 'clues' have emerged that, when adopted and implemented, help reshape inherited local churches to become more mission-shaped, and as a result become healthier and more vital expressions of Christian community. These clues resource renewal. They are not adopted primarily in order to produce *bigger* churches, but *better* churches (though encouraging signs of numerical growth sometimes result). Health and depth are better motifs than the 'mathematic' themes of addition and multiplication belonging to older church growth theory.[3] Nor do these clues represent yet another 'quick-fix' remedy for the Church (do this, then that, and *voila!* Double-sized Church!) which thankfully British Christians seem to believe less and less, if only because they have been let down so often. Rather, these hope-filled hints arise from statistical and anecdotal material suggesting that they are genetically fruitful[4] and a fertile healthy church is more mission-shaped than a barren, unhealthy church. These clues to transition and renewal, while reproducible, also require thoughtful, contextual application to the local situation, and much resolve and patience. There are no easy, speedy or painless remedies. On the other hand the clues are not very complicated or exotic and therefore are within reach of all but a few churches. There are three guiding principles, all quite obvious. Churches become more healthily mission-shaped by (a) *ceasing* to do the things that made them unhealthy, (b) by actively reshaping their lives with respect to missionary engagement with our culture, and (c) by doing the basic things of inherited church better. Becoming a healthier mission-minded church is eminently possible, and consequently the challenge to become such is real rather than the call to an impossible dream.

Worship

> The past was strong enough for the parishioners
> to feel sufficient security in one another's
> company and each other's commitment so
> that they could afford not to notice that their
> services were enabling the worship of fewer and
> fewer people.[5]
>
> *Penny Jamieson*

One 'basic' that is almost always a part of inherited church transitioning is a renewal of worship. Inherited churches in particular assume that public worship is the raison d'être of the Church, whether or not this is perceived to have an explicit missional dimension. Foundation stones declare when a church building was opened for worship, rather than when founding mothers and fathers started meeting in homes or rooms. A church is deemed 'open' when public worship takes place only monthly, on Sunday afternoons, with the building closed and locked the remainder of the time.

Mission-shaped church thinking does not ignore or relegate the crucial significance of worship, but it does approach and understand worship from a mission-minded perspective. This does not mean that every act of worship needs to be explicitly evangelistic in the sense that it is constantly challenging people to commitment. On the other hand the assumption of many inherited churches that a person *is* a fully paid up Christian simply because he or she attends worship surely needs challenging for the myth it is. Equally, not all mission-shaped thinking embraces the 'seeker service' idea that worship is primarily designed as a means to invite along unchurched or dechurched friends. Missiologists and historians are well aware, for example, that many Early Church communities did not and could not rely much upon their worship in terms of evangelism and mission. On the other hand the implicit – and all too often explicit – assumption of inherited churches that worship is designed for 'us' who regularly attend is another myth that requires exploding. Possibly the most significant 'conversion' an inherited congregation undergoes in relation to worship is realizing that it is not 'theirs'. Not only is it not theirs because it is God's, but it is not 'theirs' to manage as they want, if the way they want to manage it does not enable others to enter into worship, or jars with the desires of a missionary God.

Consequently, mission-shaped thinking about worship does not produce or promote a fundamentally different theology of worship to that of inherited church, but urges inherited church more fully to inhabit its own theology of worship. In answer to the question 'Who is worship for?' there is no dispute: worship is first and foremost 'for God'. Mission-shaped thinking conceives God to be supremely missionary and evangelist, and therefore enquires what worship of such a God will be like, feel like and consist of. The second proper answer to the question 'Who is worship for?' is that Christian worship is also 'for' worshippers in the sense that it is meant to enable human beings to worship God: Father, Son and Holy Spirit. Mission-shaped thinking therefore considers that worship is an essential, self-defining activity of church and must enable worship of God to occur in such a way that through such worship human beings become first Christian believers, then disciples. Consequently, if the worship life of a church seems not to enable significant numbers of people to worship God, and as a natural consequence flourish as Christian believers and disciples, then mission-shaped thinking tends to advocate changing worship to better meet these defining criteria rather than training people to fit into existing patterns of public worship. Like it or not, this is the natural default of most of my Christians friends, particularly those between the ages of 20 and 40.

In almost all cases of transition, the renewal of worship – of whatever style and liturgical type it may have been – tends to mean that it becomes more informal and relaxed. This does not mean that serious and profound themes and occasions are treated lightly. Nor does it mean that the untold majesty of God is reduced to infantile imagery and facile language. It does mean that worship takes on a more accessible mood and 'feel' irrespective of its theme. It better enables invitation and participation and therefore turns what is often a 'distant' event into a 'nearer', truer corporate engagement with God. Without doubt the most common characteristic of renewed worship is the presence of real joy and hope and laughter; the paradox being that this is often most authentically embodied in persecuted Christians in minority contexts.

As worship in churches becomes more mission-shaped it is also more varied and reactive to the needs of certain groups within the whole. It is no good developing a 'family service' that takes place at the worst possible time for families. In a recent study early Saturday evening was the preferred time! The music also tends to be 'better' in churches in transition. It is ironic that significant parts of the Methodist Church to which I belong, with its roots sunk deep in hymns and music, still remain somewhat 'sniffy' about worship songs and bands, but seemingly impervious to the slow discordant racket produced on many an old organ Sunday by Sunday.

Yet another feature of worship in transition is a greater level of participation and involvement by members, which is of course what the word 'liturgy' signifies – the work or offering of the people. Nor is this involvement limited to incidental or peripheral roles. Churches that become mission-shaped tend to have more lay leadership involved in 'spiritual' and significant ministries, usually to the benefit of the members involved and the whole congregation. I shall focus more fully on 'new laity' in a later chapter.

Authentic Christian spirituality

> To withhold acknowledgement, to avoid
> celebration, to stifle gratitude, may prove as
> unnatural as holding one's breath.[6]
>
> *John Burkhart*

Closely related to the renewal of public worship is the crucial, wider issue of spirituality. At a time when many people are 'spirituality hungry' the owning and embodying of an authentic, open, Christian spirituality is a key issue for inherited church transitioning to mission-shaped church and is pregnant with possibilities of renewal.

We need to note how different the present is from the past in this respect. Only 30 years ago my theological training was filled with 'death of God' secularism. I actually took bullish inspiration from the fact that there would come a time when, backs to the wall, we churches would be the only Christian outposts in a sea of unbelief. How things have changed! While Christian commentators were busy demythologizing the world, increasing numbers of western people began to remythologize their lives. It is one thing for the Church to be rejected by those for whom scientific materialism and logical positivism mean they have no time for God at all. It is quite another that the Church is rejected by a generation seeking meaning, mystery and transcendence on the basis that such is not to be adequately found in it! But such is happening today and it is a severe challenge to all churches. John Drane asserts that we have ended up with a 'secular' Church in a 'spiritual' society and urges the Christian Church today to become again a dynamic spiritual community. Identifying the rationalist mindset associated with Christendom as one of the most debilitating problems for the Church, not surprisingly inherited church particularly, he urges the adoption of non-cognitive, intuitive, emotional, non-verbal and symbolic expressions in the communication of the gospel.[7]

A conversation between famous Methodist preacher William Sangster and his musically expert son, Paul, is said to have gone like this.

'I've written a hymn.'

'Really, you must let me listen to it, father.'

'Oh, it's not your kind of hymn, Paul, it's not for "sniffers"!'

It is a challenge to the church today that we do not get too sniffy about the ragbag of spirituality that surrounds us. We must take our lead from the apostle Paul. Paul. A Jew. A Pharisee. Walking law machines. Religious ones who knew the core statutes of Judaism backwards forwards and inside out, who upheld monotheism and the rejection of all idolatry as the key bulwarks of faith. And yet Paul, such a Jew, walks into an unclean Gentile environment, sees a graven image to an unknown God and comments to his hearers how they share much in common![8] Make no mistake, today's equivalent is a clergyperson walking into a witch's coven and declaiming 'I see we share an interest in spiritual things, then!'

At enormous personal cost and risk to his own deep faith, Paul was willing to adopt the mission-shaped principle of using all means to 'save some'. Yet his costly action did not imply that any spirituality was as good as any other, he knew that all else but Christ was like trash. The same challenge faces the Church today. Those churches embarking on the journey to incarnate authentic, Christ-like spirituality are becoming effectively missional. Those churches that are not are becoming ever more distant and irrelevant to a population engaged in a spiritual search, even as they declare themselves to be spiritual communities.

Crucial to the question of mission-shapedness is whether or not church is a place where there is space to encounter God: Father, Son and Holy Spirit. I recall an old nun being interviewed on TV. She talked of church as 'Godbearing'. That is, a church pregnant with God's presence and grace, bringing forth God to people. Yet, she added ruefully, only some people. For many people, like my friends in the pub quiz team it is a fact that church has not been Godbearing at all. The nun gently suggested that the proper responses should be first, thanksgiving that church is Godbearing for some; second, penitence that it hasn't been Godbearing for many others; and third, prayerful response so that church can be Godbearing for all. Old she may have been, mission-minded she was, as are churches that seek seriously and at a cost to become Godbearing.

Alongside a host of valid reasons why so many people have chosen not to belong to the Christian Church is surely that the spiritual life of many inherited churches has a quality of 'real absence' about it. One friend states often that church constantly lives *down* to her expectations! Several friends, who rarely go to church, freely volunteer that they pray regularly, light candles and frequently spend time in quiet meditation. Mike Riddell talks of buildings in his native New Zealand being 'white anted'. Structurally they appear sound – until someone leans on one! Then the whole edifice collapses, eaten away from the inside. Alan Jamieson's book, which charts categories of those with 'a churchless faith', provides ample evidence to suggest that many leave church in order to pursue a more vibrant, meaningful and profound expression of Christian faith and life.[9] Interestingly, his book also signals that, in most instances, such people do not leap headlong into zany spirituality(ies). Rather, many remain more devoutly 'orthodox', leaving the impression that there is a growing tendency towards passionate orthodoxy emerging outside inherited churches.[10] Without minimizing what is a profound challenge today, what is being asked, fundamentally, by many, many people today, is not that the Christian Church adopts wacky mysticism but simply that it becomes more transparently Christian. The late Mike Yaconelli talked of 'standing on tiptoe' as an image of anticipation for what is to come. What a great image for a newly found Christian spirituality for today! Whatever else might be said about what a local church is, and however the roles and functions of a local church might be defined, a church where people do not meet God is no church at all.

Healthy congregational spirituality is today a litmus test for many would-be Christians. All churches 'demonstrate' and embody something. As Leander Keck puts it, 'A joyless Christianity is as clear a sign that something is amiss as a dirty church.'[11] Inherited churches in transition demonstrate that Christianity 'works' and 'works' at various levels. The 'rationalism' exuded by so many contemporary churches means that properly 'spiritual' things need recapturing. John Finney suggests that the New Testament word *mysterion* is helpful here. This subtle word does not signal a mystery that is incapable of being unravelled. Nor does it cease to be a mystery when it is made known. Rather, it is a divine mystery being uncovered, unendingly revealed by the Holy Spirit. It is a holy mystery, the gospel of Christ.[12] This deep sense of mystery, alongside a holistic, earthed spirituality that connects with the real lives of people and transforms them, is a potent combination for Christians and not-yet Christians alike. It is winsome, authentic Christian spirituality for today.

Contemporary expressions of Christian spirituality are many and varied, and all seem to produce more life and health than the now dry formalism of once-passionate inherited church life. The pre-verbal hunger for meditation, quietness and stillness, the desire among many women for more inclusive modes of life and worship, the rediscovery of our cosmos as the arena of divine purpose and design, bottom-up and hands-on, messy and struggling spirituality all seem to possess qualities that go deeper than formal religious allegiance.[13] Mission-shaped churches are not captive to any single macro-expression of spirituality, but they are churches that have begun to escape the captivity of sterile Christian spirituality.

Seven whole days, not one in seven . . .

> Churches that do not help people make sense
> of their lives and find purpose and meaning
> through their friendships and activities, in their
> meetings and homes, will find their pulpit a
> pretty sterile place, even if it produces great
> erudition and rhetoric.[14]
>
> *Martyn Atkins*

Another clue from inherited churches in transition to mission-shapedness is the growing realization that church does not live by Sunday alone. Public worship on Sundays, irrespective of its quality and vitality, cannot, of itself, carry the weight of this transition. We should not be surprised at this because Sunday worship has hardly ever fulfilled such a role. Instead, whether everything is based 'at church' or not, churches becoming mission-shaped are, if not seven-day-a-week churches or, perhaps better, 'everyday churches', much more than Sunday-only communities. Three common features of inherited churches in transition demonstrate this point.

Small groups

First, there is a marked tendency to put effort into developing small groups that work effectively in the local context. As I shall outline in a later chapter small groups can be as insular and self-serving as any other model of church. They can also be powerfully mission-shaped. It is important to realize, therefore, that simply starting up an additional group to which the faithful few turn up loyally for 'one more thing' in the life of their church is not what is required or desired. Many an inherited church retains a model of a small group long after it has died and gone to heaven. The point is not simply having small groups, but developing the models of small groups that work in a particular local context. Churches in transition think through the rationale, nature and content of a small group meeting. They also take care about the location and the timing. They have in mind a new constituency, or the extension or deepening of a present constituency, often in response to a perceived need, and they carefully shape the new group round that. One of the many reasons why courses like *Alpha, Emmaus, Disciple* and *Essence* have been so effective is that they provide a fresh model for a small group, and pose new questions about its venue, aim and content to very many inherited church 'fellowship' meetings.

Integrated evangelism and nurture programmes

The second common feature follows closely from the first. Churches undergoing transition and renewal tend to integrate evangelism and nurture events and programmes into their normal life, repeatedly or even constantly, rather than as one-offs or add-ons. Indeed in many places the benefit of *Alpha* and so on is not apparent until several courses have been undertaken. Mission-shapedness is a state of being and mind, not a 'special activity' every now and then. Consequently churches in transition to renewal also tend to provide different points of entry and engagement for different people, for example, 'points of continuity' for those 'post *Alpha*'.[15] Some of the impetus for fresh expressions of church surely lies in the fact that a proportion of those who have encountered Christ through courses like *Alpha* have been unable or unwilling to make the leap to inherited church as a consequence.

It is easy to romanticize about early Methodism. Nonetheless it is the case that a range of small group meetings existed – classes, bands, special bands and the like. Tom Albin has demonstrated how each of these was designed for (or emerged in order to meet the needs of) different kinds of people and people at different points of faith journeying.[16] The aim of each group was to provide a place where the cognitive and affective – that is, the head and the heart – aspects of religious faith met and produced greater and deeper devotion. Pursuing a regular pattern of meetings that enable different people at different points to develop in faith often leads naturally to the renewal of other aspects of the life of the local church.

Readers who are members of inherited churches may have already ruled themselves out of this section. Their church is quite the opposite of a 'Sunday-only' church. Indeed, as its members they seem to be 'down at church' most evenings what with one meeting or another. For these readers especially it is important to note that the mission-shaped factor lies not in the *number* of church meetings but in their nature and purpose. Inherited churches often have lots of meetings, but mostly of a particular type, and the type is designed to keep the show on the road and plan next year based on this year. By contrast, inherited churches in transition move towards a much more varied, 'outward' and 'deep' weekly life, focusing on discipleship and evangelism rather than endless maintenance and business meetings. Possibly more than any other single factor, more than sermons and worship, appropriate small groups and 'ways in' have kept some of my friends 'in' the path of developing and deepening faith.

Doing less – well

Having advocated that inherited churches in transition tend to be seven-day-a-week rather than Sunday-only communities it may seem strange that they also tend to do less than many other churches. But what they do, they tend to do well. They spend time and effort prayerfully discerning what their special roles and ministries are, and taking them up. This does not always come easily to them. The default model of inherited church is to be 'all things to all people', 'wholly inclusive', 'open to all'. It is a deep-rooted belief that they are neighbourhood churches and therefore 'for' the whole neighbourhood. To concentrate and focus on certain kinds of ministry, with particular groups of people, seems unnatural and almost unchristian. Yet it is this challenging realization that enables inherited churches to transition to greater mission-shapedness.

The chief momentum in deciding what to do – and, equally significantly, what not to do – is the perceived needs of people round about rather than the proclivities of the existing congregation. Many a local church has moved towards mission-mindedness and started a fresh expression of church by realizing that they are surrounded by a group of people who are untouched by their historic life and witness and have taken seriously what to do about it. In order to release the resources and energy to undertake this new sense of call a number of things usually have to be given up. This is painful but necessary and results in the 'less done better' characteristic of churches in transition.

Thicker-skinned

> Increasingly churches may become rest stops for
> people to be refuelled.[17]
>
> *Clive Marsh*

Much of this book suggests that mission-shaped
churches develop a thinner skin, a greater vulnerability and honesty. In one respect, however, inherited
churches in transition require to grow a thicker skin,
and not be affronted or easily hurt. It concerns the
way in which greater proportions of the people who
venture into inherited church are 'tasting' rather than
'joining'. In our culture of consumerism, Christianity
is 'sampled' rather than selected. Samplers come and
go, they turn up one week and disappear the next,
and inherited churches in transition learn not to get
their noses out of joint about that: 'And I went out
of my way to talk to him!' 'Yes, and he drank the
tea and ate the biscuits!' Today's samplers do not fit
the 'Christendom' assumptions of inherited churches.
Time was when if someone new slipped into a church
service more than twice (s)he was assumed to be a
fully paid-up Christian returning to a long-lost faith
and invited to join a church committee. Such assumptions can no longer be made and mission-minded
churches know that.

For some folk today, sampling is the means by
which they come to faith in Jesus Christ. It is said
that a person needs to see a new brand name many
hundreds of times before buying that particular car
or using that particular airline becomes a real possibility. Appropriating faith today is a lengthy process
of sampling and tasting. The 'wham bam' instant
conversions of revivalism, retold so reverently and
often that they became regarded as normative, the

benchmark for every conversion, take place among our post-Christian population with increasing rarity. Indeed, such 'instant' conversions are a relatively rare phenomenon in Christian history. Most evangelical Christians in past centuries, early Protestants, Pietists, Puritans and not a few later Methodists, went through months or years of anguish, doubt and guilt before 'breaking through' and coming to faith.[18] The scarceness of 'instant conversions' today is not because the Holy Spirit works less powerfully now than in days gone by. Nor is it because people today are more sinful. A more likely explanation is that the residual knowledge of the faith – the Christian memory if you like – is not what it was. Post-Christian people are starting from 'further back' and therefore in certain ways have farther to travel. This is yet another symptom of post-Christendom; people no longer have basic Christian building blocks on which to build.

In the 1950s Billy Graham could rightly say to British and American people, 'You know the gospel. You know the love of God and the sacrifice of Christ. You learned it on your mother's knee, and in your Sunday school . . . And you know you have left it behind and rejected Christ . . . I am calling you today to come back to that faith, and be reconciled to God, through Jesus Christ . . . I want you to get out of your seats, and come here to the front . . .' Today the evangelist and the inherited church can make far fewer assumptions about Christian knowledge and experience. For huge numbers of people today, evangelism cannot be the calling of people 'back' to anything, only forward into a faith they have not yet known much about at all. This sampling, then, is a necessary process for increasing numbers of contemporary people. Their seeking takes time and has multiple points of input.

It is more like doing a 1,000-piece jigsaw puzzle than being given a complete picture, if the jigsaw is ever going to reach a point when the person 'gets the picture' then local churches are going to have to become content with serving the seeker and seeing them move on. This is a proper means of witness and evangelism today. Mission-shaped churches develop thicker skins.

A thicker skin is not required merely for seekers and samplers. Today inherited churches are also visited and 'used' by people who do 'return' to church having left it – but only for a 'top up' every so often. A significant proportion of the so-called 'dechurched' population do their own version of sampling, taking another sip, making an occasional visit. Here again inherited churches in transition learn that there are more acceptable models of seeking and belonging than fully paid up traditional modes of membership and ever-present attendance. And they cope with that situation, and shape themselves so as to be most effective in it.

Youth a part

> It's not that young people do not go to church,
> it's that the church does not know what to do
> with them when they do.
>
> *Pete Ward*

Another common feature of congregations in transition towards renewal is that they commit themselves to improving provision for young children and youths, even if at first they haven't any! This is a costly business in terms of finance, space, time, personnel, providing role models and so on, but such is generally necessary. Indeed, particularly in relation to youth work, the investing congregation rarely experiences the full benefits of its ministry. One congregation facilitates 'conversion' and nurture and another, later and in some other place, receives mature young Christian adults into their midst, and there is something distinctly Christian about that. As the apostle Paul put it, 'I planted, Apollos watered, but God gave the growth.'[19] Deciding to make costly investment on this basis, however, often escapes inherited congregations, and it is easy to understand why. After all, what is the point in deliberately committing yourself to providing ministry and resources for a group that is absent? But to this 'inherited' question comes a mission-shaped answer – you commit yourself precisely because this is the case. Indeed, congregations without any provision and commitment to young people are adopting a telling body language that young people are expected to leave church as they reach puberty. One of the hallmarks of mission-shaped churches is that they are seeking to embrace those not currently 'in' rather than simply provide better things for those who already are.

Another important aspect of a commitment to provide good ministries for children and young people is that this group rarely exists in a vacuum. Most have a parent or two, a grandparent or more and friends. Contact with and provision for them is a significant corollary of the primary commitment to the young and inevitably engages the church with mission-shaped opportunities. One small, single-roomed village chapel, with a membership of nine elderly ladies decided, after prayer, to close down its midweek meeting and run an after school club. They loved it, a growing number of children loved it, and a widening number of parents, grandparents and neighbours loved it. Said one member: 'We decided that every child deserves a group of grandmas.' Here the cost was not the professional children's worker, rather it was a commitment to lay down something designed for them and take up the challenge of meeting a perceived need for others. And finding, unexpectedly, real blessing. Such is another common factor of mission-shapedness.

Growing new congregations

> . . . growth most often comes through the development of new congregations.[20]
> *Richard Kew and Roger White*

One of the clearest hints of good practice offered by inherited churches in transition is that they take very seriously the task of growing new congregations rather than enlarging their existing congregations. Put simply, it is much easier to get 10 new people to join a 'fresh expression' of church in your local church, than it is to get 10 more people to join your existing church as it is.

The crucial point is that all churches must become mission-shaped and take on fresh expressions in ways that are appropriate to their context. Four pensioners engaging in mission with four other pensioners might be entirely right for certain churches. For others it will not. This leads to the final clue about inherited churches in transition: they don't mind trying something new, and don't get put off when they make the occasional mistake.

To mull over . . .

- To what extent does your church understand worship from a 'mission-minded perspective'? To what extent has your church experienced a renewal in worship in recent times? What are the signs of this?

- 'We have ended up with a "secular" church in a "spiritual" society.' To what extent do you think that is true of your church? How might 'mission-shaped spirituality' be deepened in your church?

- Assess the significance of small groups in your church. Are they the right 'shape' and type to be most missionally effective?

- To what extent are evangelism and 'nurture' programmes integrated into the normal life of your church? What do the normal weekly/monthly activities in your church signal is most important to you?

- What would it mean in your local church to do less – better?

- How does your church respond to people who are 'seekers and samplers'?

- Evaluate the ministry of your local church with respect to children and young people? If you deem it inadequate, what do you resolve to do about that?

- Discuss growing a 'new congregation'. Why? And why not?

6

Size, Signals and Servanthood

The previous chapter identified some of the health-producing 'clues' that inherited churches in transition are now increasingly implementing to their benefit in terms of renewal and mission-shapedness. This chapter is differentiated from the previous one in that it identifies issues that I consider very significant in terms of imitating the God of mission that have not yet, to my knowledge, been the subject of the same degree of interest or adoption. The first issue deals with congregational size. The second addresses the 'signals' church sends out – with its 'body language' and its mission-debilitating kind of 'honesty' and 'perfectionism'. The last theme focuses on the need for a revised model of church servanthood and service.

Size matters

> We shape our buildings, and afterwards our buildings shape us.
> *Winston Churchill*

> Church Planting puts mission at the heart of church and church at the heart of mission.[1]
> *Tim Chester*

Over recent years it has become clear that, although the number of people attending church in Britain has shrunk significantly, and is currently shrinking much less quickly, a number of other trends are discernible. Here I outline two trends, gleaned from my own experience and impressions rather than empirical information, though there is some evidence to support these themes.[2] The first trend is a move towards larger, more 'professional' church; the second towards smaller, cell or household churches. Both trends – if that is what they are – have profound implications for older denominations with their sizeable networks of mainly small, inherited church congregations.[3]

Super-size me

The first trend I note is a slow but gathering pace to bigger and better-resourced church congregations. As the number of Christian worshippers in Britain falls overall, the proportion of those belonging to churches with large congregations has increased. One reason for this is the significant rise in large and vibrant 'ethnic' congregations, found mainly in London and other major cities. Indeed, other than certain Black, Korean and Chinese churches, Britain seems impervious to the truly 'mega-church'[4] and these churches are not exactly what I have in mind here. By 'bigger churches' I am not referring to congregations of several thousand worshippers, but rather about 300 upwards. By 'better-resourced' I mean that several staff – lay and ordained – will work within it, that it will exercise a number of ministries among different groupings, and in many cases, occupy well-maintained, even 'plush' premises. This might be an Anglican church in a university town, like Thomas Crookes in Sheffield, or a new church in a sports centre, like a Baptist church plant near Edinburgh.

Another reason for the growth of larger congregations is that the criteria that determine which church a person chooses to attend have changed. Time was when denomination was determinative. If you were a Methodist or Baptist, you knew it, it mattered, and when you moved to a new area you sought out the local church of your chosen denomination, often travelling past others to get there. For the majority of churchgoers today denomination is of little significance in this respect. Of course, there remain in each denomination those who are Church of England – or whatever – 'till they die', but for most people today denominational brand labelling comes in the relegation zone of reasons for going to a particular church. Post-denominationalism is an increasingly important phenomenon with respect to Christianity in Britain today.

Both a cause and a consequence of this phenomenon is the dilution of denominational distinctiveness, sometimes to the point of indistinguishability. Time was when an 'experienced' churchgoer could be led blindfold into a church service and know 'where she was' in denominational terms in a matter of seconds. This is no longer the case. Two movements have had a profound shaping influence on the worship life of my own denomination and others. The first is the effect of the *movement of liturgical renewal*, which not only brought much creativity to Christian worship, but also a kind of trans-denominational homogeneity to it. Liturgical renewal brought about what one friend and expert describes as 'Bread and Wine with everything'! Going to a church service, in a greater number of churches, in several denominations, became, at least in terms of its liturgical shape, an experience of déjà vu. (Even if, at the same time that bread and wine are everywhere, actually partaking of them together as Christians remains ecumenically difficult.)

The second movement has had an even greater influence upon churches of various denominations in recent times, again at some cost to older denominational distinctiveness. The *Charismatic* Movement (later to become 'Charismatic Renewal', and later still simply 'Renewal') has reshaped the map of British Christianity. Initially the Charismatic Movement was often a local breakaway from historic denominational churches. Many congregations agreed to differ, sometimes with great passion and pain, about whether or not new wine could be put in old wineskins. As a result some charismatics jumped and others were pushed. Charismatic Renewal followed a path worn plain by many earlier renewal movements and as the spiritual temperature cooled a somewhat sanitized version of renewal (re)entered the historic denominations, affecting and shaping considerable areas of their lives. Note, for example, the profound impact of 'worship songs' and their performance by a 'band' upon the worship life of congregations of every denomination in Britain in recent years.

Both the liturgical and renewal movements, then, have been 'trans-denominational' in their effects. They have contributed, along with other factors, to a situation where the denominational label of a church is increasingly unimportant for more and more contemporary churchgoers.

None of this means that 'any church will do' for people who are considering joining one. Quite the opposite. A key trait in our contemporary western context is that most of us are inveterate consumers.

Contemporary churchgoers are no exception. What has happened is that, just as older generations made choices governed by criteria such as denomination and proximity to home, contemporary churchgoers choose their church according to other criteria. Worship style is crucial, and in many respects whether it is 'traditional' or 'renewed' has become the new denominationalism. The 'standard' of worship – whatever its type or style – has also become important. Old organs with missing notes and wheezing bellows tell their own story; far better a contemporary worship group playing nicely and involving more people. Far from preaching being despised, many contemporary churchgoers treasure and value preaching greatly, and therefore the style and profile of preaching becomes a significant factor in the church they choose to attend.[5] Continuity and consistency of preacher and preaching is a common feature in larger churches.

For parents with small children or teenagers, good facilities and opportunities for appropriate meeting and worship are vital. Going 'where there is something for my children' is a major factor in choosing a church today. Consequently critical mass is important, and there are many towns and localities in Britain where one church seems to attract almost all churchgoing families with children at the expense of the others. To those who have, more will be given! The physical environment of a church is also significant: is it a sacred space? Is it warm and welcoming? Does it have sufficient going on (during the week, not just on Sundays) to meet various felt needs? And so on. All this requires resources, and therefore large churches have understandably led the way in multi-staff teams, appointing children's workers, youth pastors, family counsellors, church administrators and the like, not to mention often having several ordained people appointed to lead the church. Is it any surprise that the smaller church, often sharing a minister, often meeting in poor, cold, damp surroundings, often having a 'homogeneous' age profile (i.e. with virtually nobody under normal retirement age present), is not the natural choice for the majority, for whom resources and opportunities, rather than denominational, allegiance counts.

What are we to make of this trend towards larger churches in terms of mission-shapedness and potential renewal? Well, there is much to be welcomed. Larger congregations often offer a picture of vibrant, attractive, acceptable Christianity. These churches are 'successful' because they get many basic things right, such as some of those outlined in the previous chapter: quality worship, attractive spirituality, good leadership, wide participation, appropriate environments, pastoral care and opportunities for Christian growth and discipleship. They tend to use their resources well, investing in projects and ministries that are outward-facing, mission-focused and community-sensitive. Most are overtly committed to making more disciples of Jesus, and engage in innovative ways of encountering people in evangelism and witness. Their premises are usually tasteful, pleasant and inviting; cafés, book-rooms and prayer chapels abound. In short they tend to represent what might be called 'inherited church revamped and done well'! This is a commendation, not a criticism. It is hugely important – and encouraging – that 'normal' church can continue to flourish in this environment. It is highly significant to realize that 'come to church' models of mission continue to work for some people when what they come into is authentic and attractive. It means that, in the variety of expressions of church required for this present age and cultural context, there remains an important role for 'sizeable traditional with a renewed makeover'. The need for a mixed economy is again clear.

Some gentle words of caution must also be added. To what extent do these churches simply gather up greater proportions of the declining population of churchgoers? This is not to suggest that they do not make disciples, because most do, proportionally more so, I suspect, than 'traditional-without-a-makeover' churches. Rather, it is to note that there is also probably a significant element of redistribution of churchgoers involved here. Also, just as these churches bring encouragement, they also (inadvertently) discourage. Because if the only way of attracting considerable numbers of churchgoers is through this sizeable concentration of staff, plant, opportunities and resources, then, Lord, who can stand? Certainly not 9 out of 10 inherited churches in the land. In which case, in mission terms, we should not and cannot put all the eggs in this particular basket. Nor, I suspect, will the Holy Spirit of mission.

Downsizing

> Sometimes the very institution is a barrier,
> obscuring her deep and living mystery, which
> they can find, or find again, only from below,
> through little Church cells wherein the mystery is
> lived directly and with great simplicity . . .[6]
>
> *Yves Congar*

> Anyone who does not think small can be
> effective has never been stung by a mosquito.
>
> *Anon.*

110

The second trend is in the opposite direction, at least in terms of congregational size, and is the move to small church, sometimes very small church indeed. Although Britain has not taken up cell church to the extent some other parts of the Christian world have, nevertheless regarding church as cell is a profound shaper of church in recent years. Cell church is by definition small. If it gets too large, which many do because cells are sometimes fine examples of relational evangelism, it splits, deliberately. But cell church is not the only example of 'downsizing'. Many church plants (now often included under the umbrella of fresh expressions and emerging church) are deliberately and strategically small. Home or household church appears to be a preferred fresh expression of many church planters, whereby a family or small group of Christians move into an area or street, often long term, and live in the neighbourhood. This involves integration into the community, children in local schools and suchlike (going out), and inviting people to a range of 'normal' activities, from meals to watching football together (inviting in). Arising naturally from this long-term commitment to inculturation come about relationships, trust and authentic opportunities to witness to faith and share the gospel with others. Home church is based upon natural and organic patterns of integration and witness. Like cell church it splits when it gets too large to be what it is. It is deliberately small.

There is a subtle but significant distinction to note between 'churches with cells' and 'cell church'. In Britain, not least in the aforementioned larger congregations, cells are often an important strand of church life in that each church member is encouraged (or expected) to be a member of a cell. In this way church members benefit from the valuable blessings of both celebrating with a large worshipping congregation and sharing and learning as members of a small cell. These are effectively churches with cells, and writers are at pains to point out that the proper nature of church requires both congregation and cell.[7] Cell church in its purest form insists that the primary eccesial grouping is cell, and therefore cell – without anything else – is complete church. Home church would make the same claim. This is a particularly powerful argument when made by Christians in hostile environments, where small secret gatherings are the only possible form of church.

The potential of cell and home churches in terms of mission and evangelism is considerable. It was while at a conference in Thailand, in a group considering 'new ways of church in a global context' that I had my first experience of Chinese Christian church planters. They arrived near the end of the Conference having taken many days to reach Pattaya, a man and a woman, both in their thirties, unknown to each other, coming from different parts of China. Neither had been out of China before and I am still unsure how they came to be at the conference at all. But I'm glad they were. Both were highly impressive people but it was the woman's testimony that is particularly relevant here. She related how the Christian Church was growing quickly and gathering greater pace in her own remote part of China. Hers was the unofficial church, not the official 'Three Self' church overseen by the Chinese Communist system. A question was asked: 'Were Christians undergoing persecution in her region?' 'No, not much,' she replied, 'not if we obey the rules the authorities lay down.' 'What rules?' asked another member of our group. And this is what she told us.

112

The first rule is that Christians must not gather in groups numbering more than about 12, as any larger gathering constitutes a political threat. The second is that no transferable leadership is permitted, so each group must generate its own leadership. The third rule is that, as the state owns all property, the only place where meetings of Christians will be tolerated is in people's homes. As she related these rules our group listened astonished then spontaneously broke out laughing. She turned to her interpreter enquiring what she had said, looking embarrassed. 'They are not laughing at you,' the interpreter reassured her. 'They just find it hilarious that the three rules laid down by your Communist authorities designed to control and suppress Christianity, are golden rules of cell church!' How mischievously cunning is the Holy Spirit of mission!

There are limits to the evangelistic qualities of some cell and home churches however. When on a trip to Australia, I met a former Cliff College student and his family and was kindly invited for dinner. Over the meal I asked where they worshipped, which church. They looked a little sheepish for a moment then, gesturing round the room, said, 'Here' and told me about their home church. They, like many others had left inherited church a few years ago. It had not been an easy decision and they still felt some disquiet at the fact, but were certain that it was God's will. About six couples, most with children around the same age, met together every few days. They ate and broke bread, sang a little, and prayed together. They did not meet on a regular day, but arranged the next meeting at the end of the present one, inform-ing any absentees by telephone. 'So how do people join you?' I asked. 'How do they know where and when you meet?' 'We just invite folk along', was the reply.

Later that evening, they related this story. One day they locked themselves out and went to their next-door neighbour to borrow some tools to break into their own home. There was no one home, so they went further up the small estate to a nearby house and managed to borrow what they needed from a neighbour they had never spoken to before. Job done the tools were returned, at which point a conversation with the neighbour struck up. They then discovered that their neighbour was a Christian, had lived on the estate for over four years – as my friends had – and led a home church from his home. Seventy metres apart and neither had a clue! 'Do the home churches meet together at all?' I asked. 'No,' came the reply, 'home churches stay small, but we do chat about how it's going from time to time.'

Before leaving, I asked my hosts, 'If there's two home churches on one small estate in the suburbs of Sydney, how many folk do you think attend home churches in Australia?' They smiled at the idiocy of the question. 'Martyn,' they said, 'how would we know? We didn't even know there was one up the street until last year!' They have a point. By all statistical analysis such churches fall under the radar, whether in Sydney or Southampton. My travels suggest, however, that there are considerable numbers of Christians meeting in this way.[8] Many are refugees from inherited churches, but not all. Some are vitally mission-minded, others less so. Home and cell churches are not inevitably mission-shaped church, though they have enormous potential to be so.

In the mixed economy required today, very small models of church will, I believe, continue to be very significant indeed. Mission-shaped churches are small and real as well as big and real estate! There are few, if any, renewals in the history of Christianity that have not involved the rediscovery of the small group as a key catalyst for mission and nurture. The intimate relational qualities engendered by small groups in a 'natural' environment are a potent missionary expression of church today, as in the past. Whether through the continuation of home church and cell church, the division into cells of a larger congregation, or the continuing decline of inherited congregations (!), small church is here to stay. Each type has a place in a mixed economy, but the most effective small churches are those that are mission-shaped, are very small deliberately, and therefore commit themselves to reproduction rather than expansion.

Stuck in the middle with . . . who?

It will not have escaped the notice of many readers that this movement towards larger congregations on the one hand, and very small churches on the other, leaves the majority of inherited churches in Britain stuck in the middle of these trends. Smaller inherited churches especially, as opposed to cell or home churches, are faced with particular challenges. Most have little chance of becoming larger well-resourced church, nor do they demonstrate any inclination or desire to 'transition' to cell church or sell up and move into a couple of terraced houses. In the many cases where small inherited churches were once much larger than they are now, the issues are compounded. The legacy of 'how it used to be' and recollections of when hundreds of children filled their Sunday schools produces an instinctive and unattractive sense of fatigue-inducing failure. Just as serious, in terms of becoming mission-shaped, these churches often retain the mindset, structures and bureaucracies appropriate to a much larger congregation, with the effect that everyone in the church has several roles, and discipleship becomes largely synonymous with maintaining a no longer required infrastructure. The future health of all inherited church is uncertain in the longer term, but that of small inherited church attempting to be larger inherited church is particularly fragile. It is crucial, therefore, that work on the mission-shaped smaller church *in its own right* (as opposed to cell or home church) continues apace, and clues for how the huge numbers of inherited small churches might become mission-shaped small churches are absolutely vital.[9]

Even small inherited churches come in various types, however, and a small inherited church in the country may be quite different from one in a town. One possibility beginning to be explored is adapting the congregation-cell model of larger churches to a different context. Instead of having one large congregation, meeting midweek in cells, is it possible for a number of tiny churches in a rural or urban area to be 'cells' relating to a central, larger, co-ordinating congregation? Just what the relationship is, and how it could work needs further time to unfold. And, as with all such possibilities, there is a crucial, defining difference between enabling very small churches to 'go on a bit longer' and urging them to become mission-shaped in their own context. The former is managing decline; the latter facilitating mission.

Of course, it is not only smaller inherited churches that are 'stuck in the middle', most inherited churches in Britain are in this challenging place. They are not large enough to be 'large', nor small enough to be truly 'small'. Where do they fit in a mission-shaped mixed economy? Given the sheer number of such churches, clues as to how an inherited church of some size, like inherited small churches, become mission-shaped is vital.

Signals

> Their listening was like a huge pit waiting for his words to fill it. The trouble was that he was talking in philosophy, but they were listening in gibberish.[10]
>
> *Terry Pratchett*

Body language

The significance of church 'body language' in relation to embodying Christ and effectively engaging in the mission of God is profound. Vicky Cosstick, a lay Roman Catholic writer and researcher, challenges us to realize that church body language – like all body language – often speaks louder than words.[11] Similarly, Anthony Reddie, a Black British theologian talks about traditions bubbling under the surface of a church, rules and *modus operandi* passed on but never written down. This powerful and defining 'bubbling' narrative is the body language of a church. It is what people see and hear and 'smell' and absorb in relation to encountering the Christian Church. Therefore churches must ask, as much as they are able (being blinded and deafened by familiarity), 'What are we saying, through our symbols and gestures and witness?' When we speak, how are we heard?' 'Who are we perceived to be and what are we thought to be like?' Often what churches think and believe they are proclaiming is quite different to what is being declared by their body language. Many a church, inherited and emerging alike, assumes that its body language is approachable, welcoming and open when in fact it may be closed, covert and impenetrable. Good body language, body language that fits the grace and attractiveness of Jesus Christ, is mission critical today.

I remember going to a little chapel in the country to attend an act of worship led by Cliff College students. After getting to the village in good time I then spent 20 minutes asking directions of locals, none of whom knew where the church was. By the time I found it, with not a name, sign or noticeboard in sight, and only 40 yards from one of the people I had asked for directions(!) I was a couple of minutes after the time the service was due to start. The church was locked and I had to knock first on the door then on the windows to get in. After a short while a sour-faced man opened the door. 'The service has begun,' he stated accusingly, thrusting a hymn book in my hand. 'Sorry. The door was locked,' I said. 'Yes. Well, we're all here,' he replied and walked back into the sanctuary, leaving me alone in the entrance hall.

Writing about rapport, Sue Knight offers insights into the power of good body language, particularly in relation to communicating well with others. Though offered as good practice to individuals in business, her points are highly relevant to congregations seeking to be better shaped to partake effectively in God's mission. She talks of the importance of paying constant attention not only to what is said, but also language patterns used, voice, movement, breathing and posture. For example, people who listen with their whole body create a better rapport than those whose attention is only 'internal'. Rapport increases when a person's attention is towards the other person rather than themselves. Better communication happens when the language used is 'the other' rather than on 'I' or 'me', and when the language patterns used to respond match those of the person with whom they are speaking.[12]

A crucial part of rapport is genuine listening. Listening to the missionary God, and listening to the world God loves. For a long time inherited church has operated as if its task was to speak; it was for others to listen. In these post-Christendom times, however, listening, then responding in an authentically Christian way – in chess terms playing black to the world's white move – is better proclamation. Listening enables us to rediscover the gospel as God's good news for our context, and without listening the church can come to hold to a gospel that is not encountered as good news. Listening is powerful evangelism today. David Augsburger says, 'Being heard is so close to being loved that for the average person they are almost indistinguishable.' A Spirit-led church that truly listens will change the world.

Many churches pride themselves on their friendliness and welcome. That, they would say, is what our body language is saying. 'We're very friendly' was probably the most common refrain of Methodists commenting about their local church in the 2001 National Church Life Survey.[13] Very friendly they may well be but, as was pointed out at the time the survey was published, such a claim may not signal much at all because those who found the church unfriendly and unwelcoming were not present in church to make comment! But simply being friendly is increasingly inadequate for the missionary task the Church faces. Missionally effective churches will not only place importance on the welcome they offer, and their friendliness, but work with great seriousness to enable seekers and newcomers to become Christ's disciples. There is much more involved in this than being friendly. Bob Jackson relates a conversation between an old hand and a newcomer over coffee at the end of a service.

'It's a very friendly church,' said the old hand, encouragingly.

'I don't want a friendly church,' retorted the visitor, 'I want a church where I can make friends.'[14]

There is a subtle difference between friendliness and a community that enables deep friendships, and the latter is more missionally significant today. At the famous international missionary conference in Edinburgh in 1910, V.S. Azariah from India, one of a handful of delegates not from the West said: 'You have given your goods to feed the poor. You have given your bodies to be burned. We ask you for love. Give us friends.'[15]

If poor body language is missionally disastrous, then the body language of proper confidence – to coin a phrase from Lesslie Newbigin – is definitely missionally positive. Quiet unassuming confidence is a much better gospel than brash arrogant confidence and is much more helpful to shaping missional church. Nick Spencer tells a story of how he and his fiancée went to select an engagement ring. The first shop they went in, they looked, found the person very helpful, found a very nice ring, but decided to look further – after all, it was only the first shop. The assistant was quite happy with this and said to them, 'Please, go and look round. And when you've looked round you will see what I'm offering.' They tried various other shops. Some tried the hard sell; others were 'smarmy'. One declared that they had a special offer on a range of rings this week. 'But we don't like them,' the couple said. 'But it's a really good deal, a good investment if you come to sell it later' (!) replied the jeweller. Eventually they went back to the first shop. The pleasant assistant, the lovely ring, the price, all contributed to the purchase. Humble confidence in the gospel itself, offered in sensitive, watchful gentleness, is good church body language.

Honesty and the end of perfectionism

> We exclude many who feel they cannot/do not live up to the image.[16]
>
> *Susan Rooke-Matthews*

Graham Tomlin tells of a friend who went to church to a midweek Bible study and stumbled, accidentally, into a meeting of the local branch of Alcoholics Anonymous. Realizing his mistake but not wanting to cause a fuss he waited for a natural break in the proceedings, mumbled his apologies and left, but not before the meeting had made its impression on him. 'There seemed a measure of honesty, admission of failure, celebration of success and mutual encouragement in a common struggle that he had rarely found'[17] . . . in his local church.

'Honesty' in this sense means truthfulness about our lives, the life of faith, the life of the world and life in the church. It entails honesty about God, others and us, about experiences, life, suffering and unfathomable questions. It means putting an end to the sometimes unintentional but ultimately off-putting 'everything here is rosy' signals that churches often send out. All too often the signal heard is that only the perfect need apply. If your children are off the rails, on drugs, sleeping around, or your marriage is teetering or broken, or your spouse is a rogue or unbelieving, or you are addicted to any sort of thing or there are skeletons in the cupboards, then the signal, often subtle and subliminal, is that this church is not the place for you. There is an invisible 'sinners need not apply' sign on the door.

A friend of mine, the spouse of a Methodist minister, walked into the staff rest-room one day to find her colleague deeply distraught. She tried to console her. 'Dorothy, whatever is wrong?' she asked. It was like tugging a ring-pull on a shaken can of Coke! Out it all came: marriage on the rocks, worries about her teenage daughter, fears about her own health. When Dorothy was done, my friend asked the sixty-four thousand-dollar question. 'Dorothy, we've shared an office now for over two years. Why have you never told me any of this before?' Dorothy's response was a classic. 'I wanted to, but I knew you went to church . . . I didn't think you'd understand.'

Another aspect of this dubious honesty is the Church's tendency to signal that Christianity has all the 'answers', or when it signals a kind of facile faith as the response to simply awful situations. The truth is, as Mike Riddell comments, that 'The ambiguity and brokenness of life is simply too obvious to be glossed over'.[18] Silly triumphalism is not good witness – it isn't even good faith!

Honesty is a better policy, and today certainly opens the potential for greater mission effectiveness and renewal. I went to a church to preach some time ago where the members were renovating their church schoolroom. 'We've taken the stage out,' said the steward, proudly showing me round. Today, in terms of mission-shapedness and potential for renewal all churches need their stages taking out in terms of playacting the gospel, with a corresponding reversion to living out the reality of Christian life, which, if authentic, is its own best witness. The late Mike Yaconelli commented,

> Tell the truth. Be real. Encourage everyone to tell their story. Stop telling us there is only one story. Yes, there is only one story about Jesus, but there are millions of stories that we have to tell about finding him. Give up power and control. Stop editing out the mistakes, flaws and imperfections . . . Let others see that the church is not full of dazzling people, but rather ordinary people with dazzling stories about Jesus.[19]

In a post-Christendom culture such as ours, the positive missional effect of body language that is authentic and humble is matched only by the negative missional effect of body language that is arrogant and haughty. Church renewed for mission will be shaped by a commitment to *honesty*. It will inhabit and make plain alternative ways of seeing and living life today – and it will be real, open, invitational, messy . . . and glorious.

Level servanthood and service

> The first characteristic of a servant is that he
> lives in someone else's house, not his own.[20]
>
> *John Robinson*

> To rule, or to relate?[21]
>
> *Diarmuid O'Murchu*

The Church understood as a servant community is a common strand linking inherited church over recent decades and fresh expressions and emerging churches today. Being servants of the Servant, Jesus Christ, rightly appears to have perennial appeal. Increasingly, however, fresh expressions of servant church are appearing. The language of servanthood and Christian service remains, but its 'shape' and 'mood' is changing. The servant ministries of mission-minded churches, living in a post-Christendom context, are subtly different and distinct from previous expressions.

The Church in Britain has long used the rhetoric of being a servant church and offering service in the name of Christ, but in a certain way. At one time Christian denominations in England largely modelled servanthood on a squire dispensing charity to serfs. Free Churches, in their Victorian heydays, largely adopted a model of servanthood mirroring that of a charitable factory-owning philanthropist. It was servanthood, but of a particular sort. That sort was 'sloping', in that it was dispensed 'downwards' from 'above', to the needy 'below'. Today, such models of servanthood are becoming less useful than ever before in terms of mission, good communication and presentation of the gospel of grace.

One of the classic books about ecclesiology in recent decades is *Models of the Church* by the American Jesuit theologian, Avery Dulles.[22] Writing in the wake of the Second Vatican Council (1962–65) Dulles outlined five 'models' through which the Church's deep character is discerned. Church, he wrote is 'Institution', 'Mystical Communion', 'Sacrament', 'Herald' and 'Servant'. (A later version of his book added a sixth model, a 'Community of Disciples'.) The book was hailed as a welcome step forward in ecumenical relations as the categories included insights from Protestant as well as Roman Catholic scholars.

In some senses 'Church as servant', the last model presented in the original version of the book, is the odd one out. Dulles recognized this, commenting that all the other models gave a 'primary or privileged position to the Church with respect to the world . . . the Church is seen as the active subject, and the world as the object that the Church acts upon or influences'.[23] With the passing of time Dulles' models of church that assumed a Christendom context have receded in missiological significance. By contrast, 'Church as servant' has become hugely significant in today's missionary, post-Christendom context. Servanthood – and the service and serving that give expression to it – remain powerful expressions of Christianity and the Christian Church. But whether servanthood is a powerfully *positive* or *negative* expression of the church depends in considerable part on the particular type and mood of the service and serving. It is perfectly possible that being a servant and offering service can be undertaken with a body language that speaks quite the opposite of what is intended: we all know what a 'snotty' waiter is like, for example!

In recent decades, partly as an inevitable consequence of smaller congregations and (too?) many large, older church properties, more and more inherited churches have sought to offer their premises to their local communities. Scholars have described the later twentieth century as a period when 'mission as presence' became a major theme.[24] Many inherited churches I know offer Christian service in various and valuable ways that often belie the numerical size, age profile and resources of the congregation. Indeed, it may be the case that serving in the name of Christ has been the major expression of mission in inherited churches over the last 30 years or so. There are, however, in mission-shaped thinking terms, two inherent weaknesses with much of the service that is offered and they are not going to go away.

The first weakness concerns the body language and 'direction' in which much traditional Christian service in inherited church is undertaken. This might be described as 'downwards'. That is, most of the service proceeds from an assumed and implicit 'we have it, you receive it' mentality. It is 'sloping' service and the slope nearly always goes down from 'us' to 'them'. 'We have the room, you can use it.' Fine, but the image of landlord and tenant bubbles under the surface. 'We have the professional help, please avail yourself of it.' Wonderful, but the image of teacher and pupil rumbles. 'We have a drop-in centre, we'd be delighted to see you.' Great, but the image of therapist and patient persists. At the heart of so much service – marvellous though much of it is – has so often been a lurking air of superiority, a subliminal signal of privilege, the legacy of a recent version of Christendom.

Andrew Dutney identifies this 'down from us to you' servant mentality in his own Uniting Church of Australia. 'We are ready to care for the poor,' he states, 'to be advocates for the poor, and even to be in solidarity with the poor. But it did not occur to (us) . . . that we might one day be poor ourselves.'[25] In a combination of ways many inherited churches are moving into an era of greater poverty: in power and influence, public image and appeal, financial and personnel resources. Consequently changes in lifestyle are required. A different model of service is required today. The Church can hold to an old paternalism and regard greater poverty as a horror to be resisted as long as possible, or it can realize that this move to the margins, with much less power and privilege, enables it to stand within a deep gospel heritage and adopt a true servanthood, which is a profound expression of the imitation of Christ.

The second, related weakness of traditional modes of Christian service is that inherited churches have generally operated the 'come' model of service. 'We' invite 'them'. We meet in 'our' house. We provide the food and the know-how. We choose the furniture, the pictures and the music. As the gap widens between church congregations and increasing numbers of our fellow citizens, servanthood is going to mean living on someone else's turf, and in someone else's house. It means an end to 'home' advantages and the adoption of a 'level' rather than 'downward' model of service.

In the days when Romania was much in our thoughts many churches responded marvellously, collecting clothes, packing shoeboxes with soap and basic goods and sorting out ways of getting the stuff out there. One church in London decided to take up this servant ministry and appealed for helpers in the church notices. A few turned up to the meeting planned for the purpose, but not enough. They tried again to recruit, but although it had a largish congregation, the response was disappointing and insufficient for the task. So they placed an advert in the local newspaper and shops: 'Wanted: Helpers for organizing aid to Romania'. They were swamped with local people, many totally unattached to the church, offering to help. This caused crucial decisions to be made. They moved the planning meetings to a 'neutral' place and, in spite of being the instigators of the plan, were content that the 'officials' – the chair, treasurer and so on – represented the whole group, not the church members in the group. They ceded control, but worked happily within a larger team of people. The church basement became the repository for the stuff collected.

Many months after the project started, one Saturday morning, some members of the team, some churchgoers, some not, were filling up a van ready for the next trip to Romania. As they finished Tony, the driver, a hard-living unchurched individual slammed the van back door shut and turned to the group. 'Well,' he said, 'I just want to say that you're a great group of folk and it's grand to do this work with you. I know some of you are Christians, I'm not, I don't think. But we've been over in Romania and we all know what I'm going to find out there this time. So perhaps one of you will pray for the van, the kids out there . . . and Nigel and me as we set off.'[26]

In some older modes of servanthood and service we knew how to give, but not how to receive, or how to truly share what was regarded as 'ours'. But we must learn how. The notion of 'meeting needs' where only the needs of the one deemed in need are met belongs more to post-Enlightenment charity than Christian thinking. Christianity is more about transformation, where both or all parties are altered and enriched and converted by the encounter.

The changes required of inherited church are costly and their challenge and need must not be underestimated. The signals of effortless superiority churches sometimes adopt – often without thinking or intending it – will take a long time to disappear, but they must. Churches will become more mission effective when 'downwards' service becomes 'level' sharing, when partnerships flourish rather than patronage persists, when servanthood becomes truly that. Offering service is always easier than offering self. That is why the call to become more profoundly a servant church is so challenging.

The 'nuts and bolts' of the challenge will be different for different church congregations. Inherited churches may have to rethink radically how the gospel call to servanthood is undertaken. They may have to come to terms with the disastrous mission negative of arrogant body language which, like body odour, is most often missed by the body which has it! It may mean that in spite of still possessing some pleasant, well-equipped premises, these are not always used in expressing servanthood and service. Whether we like it or not, for many people in our communities today, church premises – however homely we have made some of them – have spoken too long and too loudly of other things to be places where level servanthood can now be undertaken or experienced. In other churches the challenge may be to reconfigure and rethink premises so that level service and true servanthood become more possible. Make no mistake; running 'your' church so that it not only *appears* to be no longer 'yours' but *is* truly no longer 'yours' because it has been returned to the missionary God for the sake of 'the others', is a profound challenge. And to do this with the smiling body language of grace is a work of God, but is the way it must be today.

Those congregations taking up the challenge of a better servanthood with respect to 'their' premises soon face the practical challenge of 'being used', especially 'providing' baptism and marriage for people not part of the congregation – and who show no interest in becoming so. An inherited church in the Midlands, soundly conservative evangelical by tradition, recently reversed its policies, existing since the 1960s, whereby baptism was 'fenced' and the marriage of divorcees not permitted under any circumstances. Now both are accepted, not because they have run willingly into some sort of moral laxity or because of changes in the minister, but because, through prayer and debate, servant openness was chosen over holy separation as their primary ecclesial and missiological *modus operandi*. This decision – the messiness of which remains a constant challenge to some – has also resulted in an increase in creative pastoral acts (such as rites for miscarriages, reconciliation of marriage and the like). Sharing in people's life-changes is now their chosen, sacrificial mode of servant ministry. Another example from a different tradition is the Baptist congregation located near the centre of a small market town that decided to use 'their' baptistery as a ball pool for children to play in while their parents went shopping. This, together with supervision and a café environment in the sanctuary, is a fresh expression of making what is normally thought of as 'ours', 'theirs'.

The challenges for fresh expressions of church are no less profound. Will they retain the hallmark of 'going' as well as inviting folk to 'come'? Being 'somewhere else', often having less to maintain in terms of traditions and premises, simply being different from inherited church in a number of ways is a significant advantage in terms of potential mission and evangelistic effectiveness – one that we must endeavour not to lose. Alan Hirsch speaks of the winsomeness of powerlessness.[27] To possess no buildings, to have no official clergy, he claims, removes much of the suspicion engendered by institutional Christianity in increasing numbers of people today. Fresh expressions therefore belie to some extent the assumption that all mission, evangelism and the like is a crude plot to get 'butts on seats' and thus collude with 'propping up the church' which is a more pervasive and deep-rooted sentiment than most in the Church care to imagine. In different ways, then, inherited church and fresh expressions have challenges and opportunities to engage in new models and moods of servanthood and service.

> The incarnation of a God of love in a world of sin, leads inevitably to the cross.
>
> *Miroslav Volf*

To mull over . . .

- What are the advantages and disadvantages of the size of your congregation, be it small, large or 'middling'? To what extent do you think the size of your congregation is mission-shaping or mission-neutering?

- What do you think the body language of your church is saying? What do you think those who do not belong to your church perceive it to be like?

- Is your church too 'perfect'? Is it 'honest'? How do you respond to the assertions of this part of the chapter?

- In what ways is listening important? Is listening enough?

- How might your church become not only a 'friendly church', but one in which people can make friends?

- In what 'direction' does servanthood move in your church? What would it mean, in practical terms, for your church to adopt 'level' servanthood?

- How do you respond to being 'taken for granted' by those who 'use' 'your' church?

7

Flesh and Blood and
Bricks and Mortar

Beauty of life causes strangers to join our ranks
. . . we do not talk about great things, we live
them.[1]
Marcus Minucius Felix

Our world is calling out for social structures that
will be more fluid and flexible, more open-ended
and mobile, more creative and adventuresome,
less self-reliant and more interdependent in their
basic orientation.[2]
Diarmuid O'Murchu

A woman was being shown round St Peter's Basilica
in Vatican City. Her friend proudly guided her from
one majestic work of art to another. 'What do you
think?' he asked after a while. 'It's breathtaking,' she
replied, adding, with an impish smile on her lips, 'Tell
me, what has all this to do with Jesus?'

The relationship of flesh and blood and bricks
and mortar – of people and property – perennially
exercises Christian disciples. Certainly, each group
of people outlined in the introduction to this book
– my aged relatives, lifelong church members in their
fifties, friends in their thirties and forties 'hanging

on by their fingernails', my 'unchurched' and 'de-churched' friends in the pub quiz league – all hold opinions about the Church in terms of buildings in relation to people.

Most Christians can rehearse some key issues relating to people and property out of their own experience. We remind ourselves often, like a mantra needing regular rehearsing to persuade us it is true, that church is 'people' not 'property'. Those who have had the privilege of worshipping – and what worship! – with Africans in huts and Cubans in crumbling tenements, as I have, know full well that the church is people. But those of us who belong to historic western denominations also know that property seems, more often than not, to dominate and configure our discipleship: 'our buildings' enable but also constrain our life as church and our ability to be mission-shaped. We know that 'our church' (understood as a place) matters a great deal to many of us. Those who have tried to suggest changes to its shape, seating or layout (even when there seemed to be no other alternative) will know that by the bruises! We know too that when 'our church' closes, for whatever reason, a size-able proportion of us simply cannot find it within us to go anywhere else. A crucial expression of our being a Christian is intrinsically connected to *a* place and for many, seemingly, no other. Many of us give and leave money 'to the church', often sizeable sums, as expressions of our gratitude for the *place* where we found God, love, perhaps partners in marriage, deep friendships and support through terrible times. Such financial generosity sometimes enables new and vital mission-shaped ministries to arise. Other times the leaving of legacies and the like enable – deliberately or innocently – the postponing of closure and the perpetuation of a status quo cushioned from the ill winds of change by a healthy bank balance.[3] I have argued elsewhere that, in missional terms, the practice of placing the proceeds from selling closed chapels into the coffers of the remaining local churches of the same denomination is more blinding and numbing than it is enabling and facilitating.[4]

Two recent conversations illustrate the people/property balancing act. The first was with members of a small, elderly Methodist congregation who, after many years of trying to 'keep up to the building', discovered yet more problems and are calling it a day. The mixture of sadness, failure and relief is almost palpable. The second, just a week later, was with leaders of a student congregation who are in the process of moving out of a local primary school, their meeting place for the last 18 months, need somewhere bigger and who long for nothing more than 'their own place', if only so as to no longer lug all the sound equipment about each week. In short, property matters. This chapter explores a little further some of the missional issues relating to people and property.

Assets: dead or alive?

The priority of 'people' rather than 'property' is now deeply rooted in much contemporary church thinking and is a topic of considerable missional significance. 'The priority of people' is, of course, a piece of shorthand for a commitment to a number of themes such as human needs, as individuals and within wider society, the relationships that shape and sustain us, and the networks and communities we create and join. The priority of people understood in this broad sense is a main theme of this chapter. 'Property' too is a piece of shorthand, and this chapter also includes an attempt to evaluate the role and importance of buildings, the issues of location and social capital and the like, from a missional perspective.

Women particularly seem to prioritize the needs, relationships and networks of people. In her book *Eve's Glue*, Heather Wraight explores the role women play in church and notes how, for most women, *relationships* are the most significant aspect of church life and Christian faith.[5] Whereas 'male' emphases tend to focus on 'doctrines', 'rules', 'office holding' and suchlike, 'female' shapers of church prioritize relationality between and among people – and God. For women, church as community and family, a place where a relationship *with* God – rather than knowledge *about* God – can be created, are the most significant features of church. Consequently women join churches and value church essentially for relational reasons: to make friends, to belong to a meaningful community, to meet with God, to pray for others, to create a healthy space for (their) children, to engage people at their point of need (including their own needs).[6] Penny Jamieson comments, 'An image that has been used to describe the way women share the gospel is that of a web. This is an image that draws attention to the capacity that is associated with women of drawing people in, and places firm emphasis on quality relationships.'[7] Nor, we should note, is this 'drawing people in' limited to the life of the church. All over the world, but particularly in poorer contexts, women trail-blaze improving community development. One writer notes, 'Empowering women is one of the keys to transforming the larger community . . . might women also be critical to spiritual transformation?'[8]

Those committed to creating mission-shaped churches must take such insights very seriously, because the emphases women bring to Christian belonging, faith and community are potentially more missionally significant and effective than those usually associated with men.

The research undertaken by John Finney in *Finding Faith Today*[9] demonstrated repeatedly the key role of relationships in the early faith journeys of people, female and male alike. Finney notes, 'Again and again a relationship with a Christian leads to a relationship with Christ.'[10] Four in every five of those people who found faith made this clear. More specifically nearly three-quarters of these affirmed that it was relationships with a *group* of Christians, rather than one Christian, who had been crucially instrumental in their own discovery of Christian faith. A healthy, open community of faith is a potent evangelistic entity.

For some, particularly members of inherited churches like my lifelong church members now approaching retirement, this increasing commitment to people often emerges alongside decreasing enchantment with maintaining buildings which, for them, at least in practical terms of time spent and money given, has been the primary expression of Christian commitment for as long as they care to remember. One minister I know refers to a local church in her pastoral charge as 'the money trap'. This disenchantment is not usually with property per se, but disenchantment with property *when it seems to be at the expense of prioritizing people*, when raising money for a new roof or boiler dominates church life for considerable lengths of time. So, when a local church is prioritizing

people in valid various ways, profound disenchantment rarely arises. It is when local churches do not or
cannot serve people in valid ways that the legitimacy
of 'keeping the show on the road' is soon brought into
sharp question, often expressed in profoundly spiritual ways, as church members experience a deep sense
of 'we-are-not-what-we-are-meant-to-be'. Mission-
minded souls tend to be unsurprised by this dis-ease,
regarding it as Spirit-initiated, designed to woo the
Church back into the mainstream of God's mission. It
is therefore hardly surprising to note that many fresh
expressions of church are characterized by a clear
prioritizing of people, especially people who have
little or no involvement with inherited churches. The
Church of England report *Mission-shaped Church*[11]
repeatedly demonstrates that such churches almost
naturally – or is it instinctively? – relate to and engage
with 'dechurched' and 'unchurched' *people.*

Consequently a *place* in which healthy relationships and outward-looking people-prioritizing occurs
is more missionally significant than whether the place
itself is 'inherited' or 'emerging'.

Coming and going

> If the church is to live in and communicate to
> a society which is now made up of a mosaic
> of cultures, it should have a mosaic of ways of
> expressing its life in that community.[12]
>
> *Robert Warren*

In terms of mission strategy – though this very phrase
suggests that a thought-through process has taken
place which is not necessarily the case – there are
churches that operate a *come* model and churches

which engage in a *go* policy. Sub groups can be identified.

Implicit inviters

For example, there are *implicit inviters*. These are
local churches where the invitation to 'come' is implicit, made simply by their continuing existence at
a particular location: 'You know where we are, feel
free to join us.' In truth, however, even this is sometimes overstating the case. I well remember the man
at a planning meeting for a forthcoming mission who
railed, 'Why do we need a mission? We don't need
new people in church. We've got enough people, just
right. Besides, I like the people we have.' But for many
more local churches, simply 'being there' is the sum
of the implicit mission strategy, if such it is. Needless
to say, such a sedentary strategy is not at the cutting
edge of mission-shapedness today and usually, in the
end, it reaps what it sows.

Explicit inviters

Then there are *explicit inviters*. These local churches
take more seriously the invitation to 'come' and articulate and embody it more explicitly. They do this in a
number of ways: perhaps by means of high-quality
noticeboards and attractive local church publications,
and often by the refurbishment of their premises,
which are designed and equipped to facilitate and
host meetings of people – and not just people meeting in worshipping congregations. *Explicit inviters*
are church communities committed to holding events
and creating environments designed for people who
do not yet belong to it. Also, very importantly, these
churches possess the confidence explicitly to invite

people to such occasions, by personal invitation, pastoral contact and developed networks, and sensitively make them welcome whenever they do turn up.

Depending on a range of factors, local churches experience a variety of outcomes from their explicit invitations. For some, it seems to make little difference – at least in terms of the number of people attending worship – which remains, for many churches, rightly or wrongly, the 'acid test' of success or failure. Other local churches successfully replenish their life, which remains largely as it was in most respects but with a new group of people belonging to it. Still other churches are more profoundly changed. Their worship, activities, small groups, nurturing events and focused ministries alter as a result of a continuing commitment to people, inside and outside their current church community. A few churches are radically altered by the outcomes of being *explicit inviters*. One church, aware that large numbers of Iranian asylum seekers were arriving in the neighbourhood, made contact with the handful of Iranian Christians and invited them to join them. They quickly found themselves with a 'parallel congregation' of Iranian Christians, who evangelized so well that the Iranian congregation soon outgrew the 'inviting' congregation. They continue to share the premises, and work at the demanding business of enabling two very different Christian communities to live together. The life of that local church will never be the same. The challenges are considerable. But they know themselves to be engaged in the mission of God as never before.

'Going' churches

The same prioritizing of people found in *explicit inviters* is a key reason why some churches develop *'go'* models of mission. This is often fuelled by dissatisfaction that inviting people to come reaches only a relatively narrow spectrum of people, who tend to be much like them. Whereas many congregations are very happy that this is the case, 'going' churches become deeply frustrated by the situation. The people who seem impervious to their invitations are the very people they feel most convicted to engage. The ones God lays on their hearts remain out of reach. As a result the strategy begins to change from 'inviting to come' to that of 'feeling the need to go'. The needs of people largely untouched by the life of the church as it is become a serious, shaping factor. The dangers of 'downward' rather than 'horizontal' servanthood outlined earlier in this book are ever present, but in terms of becoming 'mission-shaped' a local church makes a seminal decision when it resolves to *go* as well as invite to *come*.

Gentle goers!

'Going', like 'inviting to come', takes many forms, a good number of which are now termed *fresh expressions* or 'new ways of being church' and the like. Some churches are *gentle goers*. They may decide to open a café or charity shop in the local town or village. They might appoint a lay worker or youth leader to be based on a particular estate or among a certain group of people, or a multitude of other expressions. *Gentle goers* are characterized by the fact that 'base camp', from which all such activities proceed, remains located in the historic local church.

The going is 'gentle' in the sense that the journey is not too far, and there is no intention on the part of those on the journey permanently to change their place of residence.

Radical goers!

Radical goers are those Christians who, in going, do change their place of residence and make their spiritual home somewhere other than inherited church. They create 'church' in a new context or among a group of people not engaged by inherited church in any meaningful way. Some Christians become *radical goers* in response to their own sense of call, though in my experience there are fewer 'mavericks' about than critics suggest. Many *radical goers* go with the 'blessing' of a denomination or a sending local church or a legitimate leadership group. Indeed some denominations are increasingly encouraging and directing such church planting to take place. This ranges from 'pub church', fresh expressions among specific groupings such as bikers or surfers, to planting 'families' in houses on inner-city housing estates with the simple but challenging instruction to live as Christians and involve themselves fully in the life of the community over many years. One humble young Christian man I know is quite open about the fact that he cannot, should not, and must not attempt to bring people into the inherited church as it is. Consequently he is planting a Christian community, in a house, in the inner city, with his wife and young family. My twenty-something Christian son regards this as a 'normal' version of church in this context.

It is 'emerging churches' such as these that are most different from the inherited church model in a number

of respects. They are rarely located in a 'church building', with all its pluses and minuses. One church I
know of changes its venue about every six months,
determined largely by the expiry of leases and the
costs and availability of suitably sized premises in the
chosen neighbourhood. Consequently, belonging to
such a church is not associated with a place as much
as with a group of people. The activities that mark
belonging are also often subtly different from those
of inherited churches, being less about 'turning up on
Sunday' and more about being rooted in the life of the
community. And, of course, joining such a church is
highly reliant upon the witness of the existing congregation; otherwise nobody knows it exists.

The mixed economy

> Flexibility and variety are the keys to the future
> of Church buildings.[13]
>
> *Anthea Jones*

Very many churches today – locally, regionally and
nationally – are currently in transition somewhere
between *implicit inviters* and *radical goers*. Using the
example of café church, Andrew Carter, a Methodist
Evangelism Enabler observes how an inherited congregation will often start a 'new way of being church'
by rearranging the furniture in their church premises,
using lots of tables, chairs, biscuits and lights, and
listening to a speaker and a worship band. This may
well lead to a 'fresh expression of church' where the
congregation buy or rent premises in an appropriate
location and turn it into a café, providing opportunities to run *Alpha*, locate labyrinths and experiment
with 'alternative' Christian worship and spiritualities.

An 'emerging church' may come about when a few folk begin meeting in Starbucks and prayerfully wait to see what happens!

This 'mixed economy' is needed – at least for some time yet. The mixed economy of church engages different people and different groups of people than is possible for any one model of church. We are all aware that fewer people attend church as a raw percentage of the population compared with 20 years ago. But the rest cannot simply be lumped together as 'non-churchgoers'. Our society is far more nuanced than that. Some in our society belong to other world faiths and so-called 'implicit religions'; others in our society are convinced atheists. It is estimated that about 30–40 per cent of our population can be described as *dechurched*, that is, they once had dealings with church, however slight or ancient, but do so no longer. More than that, not all dechurched people are the same – far from it. Leslie Francis and Philip Richter demonstrate that people leave churches for several reasons, and suggest that the reasons for leaving largely determine the chances of their returning. Some church leavers can become 'returners' more easily than others.[14] Another 30–40 per cent of our population are sometimes described as *unchurched*, that is, people with no connection with the Christian Church at all, ever. In terms of mission and evangelism, each of these groupings and sub-groupings not only needs a dedicated and appropriate missiological response, but also requires dedicated and appropriate models of local church in which each can become disciples of Jesus Christ. This will involve a wider *variety* of spaces and locations and properties than have been found in most historic denominations and their inherited churches.

Stating that a mixed economy is needed, besides being the case, is a hostage to fortune to some Christians, particularly implicit inviters. The danger is that such people immediately breathe a sigh of relief (if they were reading this at all) and say, 'That's OK – we don't have to change anything then.' Support for the mixed economy must not become an excuse for inactivity or apathy. While it is right that we treat with scepticism the suggestion that all inherited churches (and their buildings) must be dispensed with, the view held by many Christians today – that every building is somehow inviolable, the existing model of everything is unchangeable and every church closure unquestionably a disaster – must equally be challenged. We must be more thoughtful and reflective than this. Mission-shaped thinking proceeds from the assumption that the church building *itself* must be the sacred space within which the Christian community engages in the *missio Dei*. Its shape, location, openness to change and relation to context are engaged from that crucial self-understanding.

I believe we are witnessing a shift in thinking, embodied in the ever-faster changing landscape of church life in our society, though there is yet a long way to go. Whereas inherited church has traditionally tended to begin mission thinking from a default position of its own *location*, around which mission activities revolve, mission-shaped churches are increasingly reconfiguring and relocating themselves in relation to *people*. It is the priority of people, their *identity* and *condition* – *who* they are and *how* are they – that is increasingly shaping the communities of Jesus Christ today.

Relocating location

> The gospel must be constantly forwarded to a
> new address because the recipients are repeatedly
> changing their place of residence.
>
> *Helmut Thielicke* (amended)

Parish, power and people

The connection between inherited church and geographical location needs a little more exploration. For a very long time 'church' in the West has been defined primarily in terms of buildings located within Christianized territories. This is certainly the case in England where dioceses and parishes mapped out the dominant role of the Church for over a 1,000 years. Their very existence signalled a settled Christian context. The history of the Roman Catholic mission to England some 180 years after the Reformation illustrates the point. It began with a system of *Vicars Apostolic*, leaders whose role it was to reinvigorate or replant Catholic entities in what was a clear missionary context. Once this 'mission phase' had taken root, the 'normal' system of bishops, priests and deacons and their ecclesiastical structures of cathedrals, dioceses and parishes arrived. For both the Church of England and the Roman Catholic Church in England, then, this was the 'normal' pattern of church structure, marking a 'settled' Christian territory, the *Christendom* model.

This Christendom model of church has plenty of critics today, and it is not difficult to understand why. In her book *A Thousand Years of the English Parish*,[15] Anthea Jones maps in detail how the parish system is rooted in conquest, politics and power. It was associated with taxation, and tithes to the king were worked out using parishes as a basis. The 'livings' of clergy, associated with parishes, were sometimes purchased from eminent landowners or given as gifts by them to faithful friends or families, an essentially pastoral entity becoming a political pawn. Without wishing to defend such a history, I want to distance myself a little from those mission thinkers who are totally damning of the parish system specifically and hostile towards the Christendom model of 'buildings located within Christianized territory' generally. Consequently I attempt to outline here a more temperate appraisal of some of the issues involved.

The fact is, of course, that the Christian Church has *always* sought to prioritize people and their needs. This is not some special revelation that has fallen out of heaven in the last few years. Each historic renewal of the Church has been characterized to some degree by church becoming a transforming event among people hitherto unconnected to it. This has inevitably resulted in new *places* of worship coming into being, and when sufficient numbers of such places of Christian worship arise in a region or country then it becomes markedly shaped by the Christian faith. How could it be otherwise? This is not a defence of an established, patriarchal, politicized, powerful parish system. It *is* a defence of the legitimacy – the inevitability – of 'church' being embodied in places, buildings, located geographically within a context shaped to some extent by the Christian faith: a context, incidentally, in which the greater degree the church is embodied, the clearer the *success* of the Christian mission is demonstrated, rather than its failure.

The Free Churches illustrate the distinction I am making here. Although, almost by definition, the

Free Churches rejected the diocese-parish system of the Established Church, they nevertheless came to develop variations on the Christendom 'buildings in Christian territory' model. This was a *result* of their missionary engagement with people but was not their primary *aim*. Indeed, it need hardly be said that some Free Churches made *gathered congregations of people* their only acceptable expression of true 'church'. Nevertheless, they usually named their local chapels or meeting rooms after geographical locations, and counted it an evangelistic triumph when every place of any sizeable population had in it one or more of their congregations. It was after being criticized for preaching in a diocese in which he was not licensed by the bishop that John Wesley famously declared, 'I regard the whole world as my parish.' Early Methodism was an evangelical movement highly successful in enabling people – many of whom were untouched by the life of the Church as it was at that time – to receive the love of God in Jesus Christ and become Christian disciples. The result was the emergence of Methodism as a *Connexion* – a network of locally rooted religious societies – covering huge areas of the British Isles. It is important to note, too, that the story of the English parish itself is not simply a tale of patriarchy and power. Anthea Jones makes it clear that the parish was always, from the earliest days, associated with people groupings.

Therefore, what we now refer to as historic, traditional or inherited churches did indeed make people their priority and engage in evangelism and mission to reach them. In fact churches did that very effectively, which is one reason why so very many of that model of church remain today, each required to rediscover itself in a new mission context. However, they were effective in a time when people groupings were themselves associated territorially to a much greater degree than they are today. And that is the crucial difference between then and now. The parish church was essentially church shaped by the social geography of agrarian, pre-Industrial Revolution Britain. Methodism arose alongside the Industrial Revolution and had more missionary success in some areas and among some people groups more than others. Today we no longer live 'there' to the extent we once did.

Leaders in the Church of England, Methodist and other Free Churches are well aware of this situation. It is interesting to compare the 1994 Church of England report on church planting, *Breaking New Ground*[16] with the *Mission-shaped Church* report of 2004. The 1994 report was required as much because a number of church plants crossed parish boundaries as because several hundred church plants were doing fine. Moreover, the dominant model of church plants with which this report was concerned was very much a 'clone' of the parish church. What a contrast the 2004 report is, just one decade later! It recognizes a much greater variety of mission-shaped activity going on, and many different fresh expressions and church plant species emerging. It also openly recognizes that an increasing proportion of these do not easily conform or relate to the ancient geographic system of dioceses and parishes. This is not because Anglicans have suddenly become iconoclastic about the parish. Rather, it is because the Spirit-led impetus towards engaging people outside the life of inherited church with the gospel of Jesus Christ is, for increasing numbers of Christians, taking priority over loyalty to structures increasingly recognized as now misshapen for the task.[17] Other historic churches are engaging in their own equivalent debates about the usefulness of inherited shapes in relation to the call to participate in the mission of God.

A key question facing all inherited churches in our society today, then, is this: what expressions of church are best fitted to engage in God's mission today, and where are they best located in order to do that? Nor is this an academic exercise because, once the way ahead is discerned, inherited church denominations must follow faithfully and courageously – at every 'level': national, regional and local. My own thoughts are below, offered humbly and warily because I am well aware how easily brief suggestions about hugely complex issues can be made to sound ridiculous. Consequently I am more concerned with principles than prescriptions.

Serious sensitive stocktaking

> There are some communities with several
> churches all serving the same area, whereas
> in other burgeoning new areas there are no
> churches for the new communities.[18]
>
> *Christopher Walker*

At every level the leaders of inherited churches – both within their own denomination and ecumenically – must continue to 'stock take' with some rigour. Mismatches between the provision of *appropriate* expressions of church and centres of population must be taken seriously. Where there is a sizeable population with no *appropriate* expression of church it must become a matter of some priority to plant one. Where several churches offer the same model, distinction and difference must be encouraged. Great care and careful listening must be undertaken in working out what is appropriate in quite different and often very localized contexts, but the guiding principle is the matching together of the prioritizing of people with an appropriate expression of church.

The reverse situation is trickier. What are appropriate responses to situations where churches are over-supplied in relation to the population? Again, contextual factors are crucial. Ten churches in a small town of 1,000 inhabitants is a quite different situation to one church in a village of 100 people. All the churches might be exercising appropriate, valuable ministries among different small groups of people. If they are not, when high numbers of similar churches are set in largely depopulated areas, then things tend to be sorted out naturally! It is appropriate to adopt mission-led criteria that determine if continued denominational resourcing and input shall be put into every local church. It is not inappropriate to consider if a local church can transition to another kind of church needed by, but not yet offered to, a very small community. Nor is it wrong to leave a contented church congregation to live on or pass away in peace, while actively developing and resourcing another needed expression of church in the same community.

The place of church is more than geography

Today well under half of the population establish relationships on the basis of geographical proximity to others. People . . . today relate sociologically more than geographically.
They relate to those with whom they perceive

themselves to have something in common more
than to those they live next to.[19]

Robert Warren

The *location* of church today, especially if it priori-
tizes people who do not already belong to it, has to
do with much more than identifying 'Christianized
territory'. I heard recently of a 'train church'. Apparently a number of commuters into London meet every
weekday morning and evening, sharing stories, prayer
and Bible study material. The number of 'churches'
arising in cyberspace, among computer-networked
communities, is another example of 'relocating'
church today. The questions such 'churches' pose for
those who require church to be located in some existing ecclesiastical territorial pattern or network are
intriguing. Increasingly contemporary western people
do not function *only* geographically and certainly
think less and less in terms of parish boundaries. As
J.G. Davies put it, somewhat prophetically, over 40
years ago:

> There is a general trend in modern western
> life to be acknowledged, which may issue
> in the breakdown of the congregation-type
> based upon residence – the parish is no
> longer the world of the individual labourer
> or professional . . . In work and leisure (s)he
> is mobile. Whenever this situation exists the
> residential congregation may be something
> of an anomaly. No doubt it has a part to
> play in ministering to the private sphere of
> human existence, but the Gospel addresses
> the *whole* (person) the *whole* of . . . life.
> This pinpoints the present structural crisis
> of the Church. If it is truly to participate in

> mission, it must devise new and pluriform
> structures that will enable it to engage with
> the new structures of modern society.[20]

I recall asking one minister of a church in a commuter town on the edge of a British city, 'How many people live here?' His intelligent reply threw me a moment: 'What time of day?' I asked him to explain. 'At 4.00 a.m., when nearly everyone is in bed, there's about 17,000,' he said, 'but from 7 in the morning until 7 at night, about 6,000.' This is not an unusual situation. What is unusual is that Christian people are beginning to realize more and more that such factors profoundly impact mission-shaped thinking about church today. Today we relate to each other sociologically, in terms of work, travel, interests and leisure. This gives meaning and shape to our lives just as certainly as where we happen to 'live'. As Ulrich Beck puts it: 'To live in one place no longer means to live together, and living together no longer means living in the same place.'[21] Fresh expressions of mission-shaped church tend to respond positively to such social developments.

People like us

The move from geographically rooted congregations to sociologically constructed groupings raises afresh the contentious issue of homogeneity (that congregations consist of people who are very much alike in certain shaping ways). Church homogeneity is not a new issue. Critics and supporters of church growth theories have debated its merits and failings for a long time under the somewhat unwieldy phrase 'the homogeneous unit principle' (HUP). The origins of this phrase lie in the work of Donald McGavran (though he himself made less of it than some of those who followed him). McGavran, a third-generation missionary to India, was concerned at the lack of success in terms of Christian conversions and began to research how, in an authentically biblical way, people groups – such as castes and tribes – might be brought to Christian faith: in short, how churches grow. Influenced by Roland Allen's book, *Missionary Methods: St Paul's or Ours?*,[22] he noted how St Paul appeared to focus his mission on people groups, and particularly those who seemed to be, either through the revelation of the Spirit or human observation, most open to the Christian gospel. Like Allen, McGavran was therefore critical of the missionary methods adopted by most missionary societies of the day, which he regarded as an expression of a western individualizing of the gospel whereby people were plucked out of their context and westernized in order to be Christianized. This, he contended was a kind of racism and argued strongly for indigenous churches. Put simply, McGavran asserted that people should not be taken out of their people groups or social or cultural contexts in order to become Christian. But he went further than this. Using the empirical evidence arising from his essentially sociological approach, he observed that 'peoples become Christian fastest when least change of race or clan is involved'.[23] Later, and after becoming founder of and professor at the School of Mission at Fuller Seminary in California, this observation was sharpened up and presented as the HUP, namely that 'People like to become Christians without crossing racial, linguistic or class barriers.'[24] Or put at its most basic, people like to join and belong to churches consisting of people like themselves.

154

The argument about the HUP is fundamentally about the relative merits of practice and theory. In practice few dispute that almost all churches, of many types and in many places, are shaped by the HUP. Descriptively that just seems to be how it is. In terms of 'theory', however, as believers in a gospel that asserts: 'There is no longer Jew or Greek, there is no longer slave or free, there is no longer male and female; for all of you are one in Christ Jesus',[25] Christians have intuitive problems with the HUP. It can too easily rationalize apartheid and social inequality. It seems to excuse too readily local churches that fail to embody gospel community at a profound level. Consequently, even those who recognize the pervasive nature and practical appeal of homogeneous congregations regard it more as a description than a prescription. Yet pervasive it is, and at a number of levels, some of which seem more inevitable than corrupt. All of us choose churches for some reasons: the worship style, the theological and ecclesial 'mood', denominational identity, size of congregation, even the main language spoken in it.

There is a paradox here. At a local level the more congregations are made up of 'special interest' groups – youth church, students, bikers, surfers, a church meeting in a gym on Tuesday evenings after a weights' class – the greater the tendency to homogeneity, with very many congregations catering for 'people like us', with our common interests or hobbies. Many fast-growing churches in the UK today arise naturally out of particular ethnic populations. Yet, at a macro level, throughout a region or a denomination, there is a much greater variety of types of congregations existing today, which actually produces more diversity in overall terms – the opposite of homogeneity. Consequently some suggest that it is just plain stupid to expect heterogeneity in small groupings, but not in a denomination or in a regional network of churches.

Hostility to homogeneity is a commonly cited reason for rejecting mission-shaped church thinking and is not without force; few mission-minded thinkers deliberately fly in the face of gospel principles, but then the biblical material is far from monotone in this respect. God's creation is wonderfully various, but is also chock full of homogeneous species, cultures and peoples. Jesus Christ is Saviour of all, but comes as a man, a Jew, in a time and place and culture. There is what theologians call the 'scandal of particularity'. It is not, however, an 'either/or' situation. Inherited churches are hardly known for their intrinsic heterogeneousness. I recall a serious and well-intentioned discussion with a small Methodist congregation of people who took great pride in their own claim to openness to all and to embracing difference, and a correspondingly dim view of some other local churches deemed to be homogeneous in one way or another. All 16 of them were female and retired! Very many inherited and emerging churches are shaped by the homogeneous unit called 'the way we do it round here' and those who do not or cannot conform to this implicit, invisible, but hugely powerfully shaping force sometimes constitute a throughput akin to a lemming farm! Their exit is then, incidentally, deemed to be a lack of commitment or faltering faith. A sinister form of homogeneous unit – even as we protest it is not one – is where different people are required to shape themselves to our style, learn our language, accept our traditions – becoming, in Chuck Hunter's memorable phrase, 'church-broke', as one would 'break' a horse. Indeed it is variations of such inherited homogeneity writ large that results in the missionary situation in which we now find ourselves, where huge rafts of a needy population cannot find a home in what we have made 'church'.

The bottom line is that authentic heterogeneity – which must be sought, and is truly wonderful gospel when it arises – is not easy. Perhaps that is why it is so rare. Even local churches that appear to be more heterogeneous often have people on the margins living uncomfortably with the dominant shapers of the congregation. White middle-classness dominates many a church where such people are but a subgroup. Certain imperialistic cultural mores shape many a multicultural congregation. So this is not at all easy, nor is it an issue that pertains only to either inherited or emerging churches. It challenges us all.

I believe we require different models of local church other than those driven by idealistic views about local communities and nuclear families. That is the lasting value of youth congregations, recovery groups and the like – homogeneous though they are to some extent. They create genuine communities minus traditional dogmas about parish. Yet we will need to become more creative and nuanced still. Sensitive, responsive, locally earthed *diversity* will be the order of the day, but not necessarily within each congregation, because, in the end, the homogeneity that arises as a result of missional and evangelistic engagement is to my mind a better version than that homogeneity which resides where there is none.

Not throwing out the baby with the bathwater

In spite of this undoubted move towards sociological rather than geographical groupings there remain cogent arguments for the continued validity of geographically based community churches. Fresh expressions of church that stand outside traditional boundaries and notions of parish are commonplace, those that stand fast and loose to *any* notion of geographical location remain rare. The call for a mixed economy is not a call to replace one virtually monopolizing church model with another. In a paper 'Losing our Space, Finding our Place: The Changing Identity of the English Parish Church', Martyn Percy argues for a reappraisal of the parish system of the Church of England. He suggests that, rather than simply accepting the common split of the *parochia* and the *ecclesia*, new ways must be sought whereby 'local' churches engage afresh with people and contexts on many different levels. The guiding principle of the parish system, to incarnate the life of God within a given community, remains desirable and missiologically fertile. *Ecclesia* must continue to find proper *parochia* and this will necessarily include geographically located churches as a continuing model in the mixed economy. Robert Warren puts it cogently: 'The parish system has served the church well in continually alerting it to its mission to the whole community and to the structures of education and welfare in that area. However, we will need to continue to be committed to the principle of service to the wider community whilst learning to be flexible about how it is achieved.'[26]

The importance and evolution of local church community ministry is a major theme of Ann Morisy's writing. She, more than most, reflects intelligently upon the place and role of the church in post-Christian Britain. A severely weakened welfare state, together with signs of a renewed political commitment to local communities as crucial units of social cohesion, provide the context for her assertion that contemporary society needs local churches just as churches need missionary engagement with local communities. However, because Christendom is dying the older modes of community ministry and mission must change. 'The new environment to which the Church has to adapt is characterized more by our powerlessness than by our power', she states, and this 'enables us to move closer to the poor, and with this, our understanding of the Gospel has been transformed.'[27]

The 'big idea', according to Morisy, is 'Social Capital' which is 'extremely significant to the Church – and the Gospel, because social capital is essentially about trust and the ability and willingness to cross boundaries between strangers.'[28] She differentiates between *bonding* social capital, which essentially glues people together (rarely a bad thing itself), and *bridging* social capital, which 'journeys out' beyond its own (homogeneous) bonded grouping or network, and seeks to generate trust with 'strangers'. Both types of social capital are important, but bridging social capital is not only rarer but also crucial for developing healthy social communities today. Churches, she asserts, are 'unsurpassed generators of bridging social capital.'[29] Traditionally, bridging social capital was expressed through the 'parish' and its 'commitment to those beyond the congregation'. The more recent inability of 'parish' to perform this vital function leads increasingly to the view that it is anachronistic, unsustainable and unfashionable and should be discarded. Instead, Morisy suggests a 'fuller evaluation' of parish, parish reconfigured for new purpose as a better way. This will involve long-term presence in a community, depth of knowledge about a community and a deep, active pastoral commitment to the whole community. It will involve commitment to the slow process of trust building between different community groupings, the honest facing of facts and historic biases. It will involve engagement with community activities, encouraging shared and wide participation from a position of mutual needs and responses. It will involve the forming of structures that encourage dialogue and conversation between people who have not talked to each other before. It will involve identifying and sharing the connections that do already exist between diverse, local people and using them to advantage. Morisy comments, 'The fact that churches have been present in a community for decades, if not centuries, counts for something. No other agency will have the voice and depth of history that the Church represents, and the local church must harness, and be *allowed* to harness, this asset wisely and generously because it cannot easily be replicated.'[30]

Configuring local church life around building social capital today challenges many historic *modus operandi* of the church. One is the commitment to 'needs meeting'. Virtually the raison d'être of earlier generations of Christian community service, 'needs meeting' must now be recognized as inadequate and dangerous. Inadequate because it fails to recognize that local churches must move from a 'we give, you take' relationship to a more mutually enriching partnership. Dangerous because an 'unfettered and unthought commitment to community involvement or community ministry could contribute to an undermining of the local church itself'[31] in the sense that such ministry may not embody the quintessential 'value-added' missional factor that the Christian Church can – and must – bring. Morisy writes:

The availability of churches and church halls
for use by the wider community is one of the
taken-for-granted aspects of British life. . . .
This easy availability of church halls and
church centres is one of the underestimated
contributions by churches to social capital
and social cohesion in many local communities. Churches have proved more successful
than local authorities and tenants and resi-
dents' groups at running and maintaining
facilities for community groups. However,
what churches have been less successful at
is tracking and articulating how this open,
and often generous access, translates into
mission. [32]

Ann Morisy's work is a timely reminder that location
– place and presence – remain hugely important. That
being the case, the need to design and reconfigure
more appropriate models of geographically rooted,
community-located church is vital to Christian mission in our increasingly post-Christendom context.

The vision of the Christian community

Jesus did not write a book, but formed a
community. [33]

Lesslie Newbigin

The forming of Christian community is a foundational
theme in mission-shaped church thinking. People
are prioritized, but particularly in terms of their life
together as a missional community of disciples of
Jesus Christ. A *good* Christian community is quite
simply the most potent God-glorifying, evangelical,
missional, nurturing and renewing entity known to

us. I emphasize the word 'good' because, although it can be argued that all churches are Christian communities, they are not all necessarily *good* Christian communities. When is a Christian community a good Christian community? Throughout this book I have contended that a good Christian community is shaped essentially by living in and for God's mission, embodying Christ the servant Saviour and being constantly open to the renewing of the missionary Holy Spirit. As a consequence, church possesses some recognizable characteristics, traits and practices. In this last section I want to explore a further aspect of good Christian community by drawing upon work by Gregory Jones and Michael Cartwright who urge 'a recovery of the kinds of *communities* in which, under the guidance of the Holy Spirit, Scripture can be properly read and interpreted, our histories as a people can be told, and theological dialogue can be fostered'.[34]

Christian community so defined, assert Jones and Cartwright, stands in sharp distinction from the more general understanding of 'the believing community' as 'any gathering of people who understand themselves as in one way or another "believers" '. Put simply, many such communities are less than they should be, as they exist (seemingly quite happily) in an individualistic or collectivist society, but 'do so at the price of failing to embody an alternative to the destructive forces of individualism and collectivism.'[35] To quote Stanley Hauerwas, 'Alas, in leaning over to speak to the modern world, we have fallen in.'[36] This cultural captivity and capitulation means that such communities are less *Christian* communities than what Robert Bellah terms 'lifestyle enclaves',[37] places where people go for 'aesthetic' or 'therapeutic' reasons and rejoice to find people like themselves. Ultimately such groupings lack the 'substance of community' because they are not locations for the theological discourse and interpretation of Scripture that is necessary for the transformative power of the gospel to take place.

Jones and Cartwright present an alternative, more substantive understanding of Christian community, defined not simply because it gathers, but by a recognition that community arises through 'particular practices skills and habits',[38] and they go on to suggest what these might be.

- First, Christian community means engaging in 'shared practices and disciplines: learning to pray, fast, read Scripture and celebrate the sacraments together, learning to care for one another's needs, ranging from the material needs of food and shelter and money to the personal needs of trust and affection; learning to be willing to be forgiven and reconciled and in turn to practise forgiveness and reconciliation.'

- Second, it entails a 'refusal to be captured by the dominant images and ethos of the wider society' or 'construe community in terms of managerial effectiveness and efficiency, therapeutic satisfaction, or aesthetic enjoyment', rejecting the view that 'life is about "looking out for number one" '.

- Third, to 'recover biblical and theological notions of community and discipleship'. This includes 'diversity of gifts within a unified Body', 'emphasis on discipleship as morally transformative friendships' and a recovery of the belief that to find your life you must lose it, 'that discipleship entails a cruciform life, a life patterned by the cross of Christ'.

163

- Last, 'Christian community is marked by the recognition that the achievement of Christian community comes as a gift from the Holy Spirit', that it is through the 'development of particular practices, habits and dispositions' under the leading of the Holy Spirit, that groupings and 'lifestyle enclaves' become Christian communities.[39]

Christian communities understood in this way challenge inherited churches and emerging churches alike. As Richard Keyes has noted, the twin tendencies of church being and becoming a 'chameleon' in relation to its cultural context on the one hand or a 'tribe' and ghettoized on the other remain equal and real threats to authentic Christian community.[40] The polarizing tendency of both chameleon and tribe models – those who 'opt in' in a prevailing cultural context to the point of invisibility and those who 'opt out' of it to the point of irrelevance – are equally damaging, and the need for Christian communities that are engaged and distinctive and authentically Christian *at the same time* is a critical challenge in these days. Inherited churches are challenged because a key reason why so many people have rejected and left them is quite simply because they have so often failed to be such communities. Often there have not been enough calories about to sustain discipleship or belonging. Emerging churches are challenged because, with all their vitality and commitment, unless they become communities that are *Christian* and produce Christian *disciples* they will fail at the deepest level to be true *churches* at all. Beyond all talk about buildings, location, geographical and sociological groupings, even people as autonomous individuals, the creation and nurture of Christian disciples in the

context of good Christian communities is the core
business of mission-shaped churches.

To mull over . . .

- In what ways do our buildings enable and
  constrain our life as church and our ability
  to be mission-shaped?

- In your church life does it seem as
  if 'people' or 'property' is normally
  prioritized?

- If women are influential in shaping
  church, what might men contribute that
  brings about greater mission-shapedness
  in your church?

- What would someone need to know or
  understand in order to feel comfortable in
  your church?

- Where would you locate your church
  on the spectrum of 'implicit inviters' and
  'radical goers'?

- If church had never existed and you had
  to invent it now, what would it look like?

- What are the pros and cons of
  geographically located church in terms of
  mission and evangelism today?

- In what ways could your church be described as a 'homogeneous unit'? Apart from meeting in church, what do the members of your church have in common?

- How do you respond to the 'vision of the Christian community' outlined at the end of the chapter?

8

Sharing Faith and
Making Christians

It's time to go back to the drawing board and
begin to reconceive Church as a by-product of
following Jesus rather than as a multinational
with a Gospel franchise.'[1]

Mike Riddell

Show me a Christian and I'll become one.

Mahatma Gandhi

Sharing faith

The best argument for Christianity is Christians;
their joy . . . their completeness. But the
strongest argument against Christianity is also
Christians – when they are sombre and joyless,
when they are self-righteous . . . when they are
narrow and repressive, their Christianity dies a
thousand deaths.[2]

Sheldon Vanauken

There can be few words that strike greater fear into
the hearts of many Christians today as the word
'evangelism'. Rebecca Pippert commented that most
people wouldn't do it to their dog![3] Repeatedly in
recent surveys the area of discipleship about which
Christians feel most unconfident and ill-prepared

is evangelism. Yet, in spite of this, bearing witness, sharing faith, and making followers and disciples of Jesus Christ, are potent forces for renewal, both in the Church and in the lives of individual Christians. Existing disciples engaging in evangelism, and new disciples who are the 'fruit' of evangelism, are both renewed through obedience to God the evangelist, who calls the Church to make Christ known and offer him to everyone.

No wonder, then, that the 1990s were designated a Decade of Evangelism. It filled a perceived need to propel evangelism up the agenda of the Christian churches in Britain and promised renewal as a consequence. If the intention of the Decade was to revive certain older models of evangelism, however, then it was pretty much a flop. To be sure, gifted evangelists continued to minister effectively to large groups throughout and after the Decade, just as they had before it. But, if anything, the Decade laid to rest rather than revived the 'crusade' model of evangelism. Gavin Reid, deeply involved with Mission England – a series of meetings by Billy Graham in the 1980s – expressed his conviction that these events drew to a close the era of mass crusades in stadia as a major method of evangelism.[4]

If anything, then, by the end of the Decade several traits had become clear:

- Some of the older models of evangelism were increasingly abandoned or at least less enthusiastically advocated,[5] cold call door-knocking, for example.

- There was a genuine seeking of new and better models of evangelism (by now often described as

168

'faith sharing' (itself a sign of the unpopularity of the original term).

- Mostly, these new models of evangelism became identified as a ministry of the mission-minded church congregation or the individual Christian bearing witness and sharing faith, rather than merely that of the professional evangelist.

- As a result, the number of 'evangelists' in an older formal sense probably fell, while the number of people appointed to be 'evangelism enablers' – those who, volunteers or 'professionals', facilitated evangelism for both congregations and individuals – grew considerably.

- In this new context emerged a renewed and welcome interest in the ministry of 'the evangelist', particularly in terms of locating that ministry within the local or national church rather than outside it in the form of an autonomous 'para-church' or 'evangelistic' organization.[6]

Today, the suggested means and moods whereby 'faith sharing' and 'presenting the gospel' are undertaken are significantly changed from those of only a generation ago. We are beginning to retrieve an older, broader and deeper palette of faith-sharing possibilities, brought about in considerable part by the increasing demise of Christendom and modernity. Over the last four centuries or so, evangelism and mission have often been distinguished from each other. Evangelism was the reviving or reawakening of existing Christians and Christian communities, making evangelism essentially an activity within a 'Christendom' context, whereas mission was the activity of going and making disciples in a non-Christian environment, an activity extending Christendom. Today that distinction is increasingly redundant and, in fact, hampers better evangelistic, missionary engagement. Evangelism in the post-Christian West necessarily involves elements closely associated with historic mission activity, and mission activity necessarily includes evangelism.

A key challenge today is the reintroduction of 'new evangelism' to inherited churches which, ironically, often tend to cling protectively to the old understandings of evangelism in order to continue to castigate it and reject engaging in it. It is important to make clear that evangelism is not about filling pews or a well-honed 'system' – like following 'spiritual laws', or merely preaching, or a one-off event led by an invited stranger or an optional extra for Christians who 'like that sort of thing'. Evangelism is good news about Jesus Christ, focused upon God the Father and the kingdom, wholly reliant upon the Holy Spirit.[7] Crucially, however, evangelism is a permanent, required element of the *missio Dei*. The missionary God is an evangelist, and intends the Church to heed the commands of Christ to declare faith, invite others to share it and make disciples. It is a joy and a privilege rather than cold duty or responsibility. When churches revisit and engage with evangelism today, they take a major step towards the greater possibility of renewal.

What, then, does 'new evangelism' consist of? A question to which my answer is: 'many of the main themes with which this book is concerned'. These things constitute 'new evangelism'. Consequently the brief collection of overlapping and cumulative statements I offer here simply echo key themes from this book and outline principles and values that, though expressed differently, apply to both congregations and individuals alike.

- *Being comes before doing (but 'doing' is not optional).*

Lifestyle and witness is powerful evangelism. What is seen is as important as what is heard. That's why, when you are in hospital, the nurses pull the curtains round the bed rather than give everyone else earplugs! Christianity is much more easily received as good news when it is attractively packaged, both in individuals and churches. I heard of a funeral service for a man who had spent a long time as a Christian missionary in Africa. The service was attended by some people from the area in Africa where he had served and they were invited to say a word. They talked of his hard work, love and care. 'He became known throughout the area, by everyone, not just Christians,' said one, 'as Mr Jesus Christ man.'

- *Lives and lips are in agreement (living it and telling it are indissoluble).*

Mahatma Gandhi apparently once said to Christian missionaries in India, 'You try so hard at it. Just remember that the rose never invites anyone to smell it. If it is fragrant people will walk across the garden and endure the thorns to smell it.' Roses and churches are different, however. To do what roses do naturally because they are truly roses is different from doing what churches do naturally because they are truly church. The Christian Church is the chosen partner of an evangelist God, and therefore doing evangelism is not optional. So lips speak, appropriately, sensitively, graciously.There are many right times to talk of God, of Christ, of the Spirit, of faith,

171

to bear honest, humble witness to the gospel hope within.

- *Being vulnerable is as important as being strong.*

The evangelistic power of bearing honest witness to faith in vulnerability today is profound. A lay preacher I know has struggled with multiple sclerosis for several years. She said recently, 'When I was well I used to witness to my faith at work and preach in church, and I don't think anyone gave a hoot. Now I talk about Jesus from my wheelchair and they hang on every word.' Today's most effective evangelists are not shiny-suited, slick-speaking go-getters. They are 2 Corinthians 4 people, those who have treasure in jars of clay. Cracked jars of clay that simply cannot prevent what is within from leaking out.

- *Being real is better than always being right.*

I know many Christians who have won an argument and lost a friend. Jesus often seems to place priority on keeping channels open over winning arguments, almost as if he wants to avoid humiliating the other person, from boxing them into an 'I win, you lose' situation. New evangelism distinguishes between the kind of cocky, confident certainty of a particular kind of Christian witness of yesterday and the quiet, confident 'faith certainty' of today and tomorrow. Faith certainty is the 'I believe it to be so and am staking my life on it' witness, rather than 'I'm right, so you'd better believe it.' This principle extends to the weightier business of 'apologetics', which now must be regarded increasingly as a vital kind of pre-evangelism.[8] A gracious rather than an aggressive faith confidence must characterize the coherent, intellectually robust articulation and defence of Christianity, in the sea of clamouring voices that make up our contemporary society.

- *Being close is better than being distant.*

The most significant things in life are done close up rather than far away. Whispering is the language of intimacy. Conversation is the language of friends. Both are better than evangelism by megaphone. Brian McLaren talks about evangelism as dance. 'Dance is not about winning and losing,' he says. 'When the music ends, you don't sneer at your partner and say, "Gotcha! I won that dance, 7 to 3!"'[9] Then he adds, 'Can you see how "trying to convert" someone is inconsistent with a relationship? It is wrestling, not dancing; an argument, not conversation; win-lose, not win-win; sales and conquest, not friendship.'[10]

- *Travelling together on the journey is as important as arriving together.*

Evangelism today does not usually materialize out of thin air, but out of experiences and stories shared and trust engendered. Ed, a Christian, himself bereaved several years ago, worked at a friendship with Daniel, a neighbour and not a professing Christian, whose wife died suddenly. They began to go places together. Daniel introduced Ed to football matches and curries and Ed introduced Daniel to ramblers and his local church. Their mutual friendship deepened over time. They both attended a church weekend away and at a quiet, intimate evening service the leader invited people to (re)commit themselves to Christ. Ed went forward and knelt at the rail, then became aware of his friend kneeling beside him. That night Daniel committed himself to Jesus for the first time. He said to Ed afterwards, 'We go everywhere else together, so I wasn't going to let you go to meet God on your own!'

- *Inviting people to believe is inviting people to belong (and vice versa).*

Belonging and believing, then, go together. Church, however humble it is, remains a community of potent evangelism. Conversion that is merely mental assent to various doctrines or the rehearsal of set formulaic prayers is a poor model of Christian commitment. Evangelism, defined by Billy Abraham as 'that set of intentional activities which is governed by the goal of initiating people into the kingdom of God for the first time'[11] requires the Christian community to be a context of challenge, ritual, initiation, experience and friendship. Believing without belonging and belonging without believing are both defective discipleship. Evangelism necessarily involves both. Put simply, evangelism today is incarnational, relational and authentic.

Making Christians[12]

> *Discipleship* sums up Christ's plan for the
> world. Yet for all its brilliant simplicity, it is the
> one approach that most western churches have
> neglected. Instead we have reports, commissions,
> conferences, seminars, missions, crusades,
> reunion schemes, liturgical reforms – the lot.
> But very little attention has been given to . . .
> discipleship.[13]
>
> *David Watson*

I contend here for something straightforward yet profoundly challenging. Namely, that a crucial means by which authentic, mature disciples of Jesus Christ will be made in the West in the early twenty-first century will come through revisiting, appropriately revising and innovatively implementing the distinctive way of making disciples developed in the early centuries of Christianity. This was known as catechesis.

Catechesis – what is it?

Catechesis was the term given to a comprehensive process of disciple-making popular in the early centuries of Christianity. Various models of catechesis were developed over the first four centuries of Christianity and differences in emphases, content and length are evident. Nevertheless 'classic' catechesis involved several discernible phases, beginning with the enquiry of a 'seeker' and ending with a mature, fully initiated Christian. I sketch out here a somewhat rosy and romantic, but nonetheless essentially accurate, composite picture of Early Church catechesis.[14]

Gathering seekers

'Enquirers' or 'seekers' (yes, the Christian ancients did use that phrase – it isn't an invention of Willow Creek!) were gathered together in a group and shared in what might now be regarded as 'pre-evangelism'. Seekers were welcomed by the leader (the catechist), introduced to each other and to some Christians who also shared in the group. The balance of seekers and Christians was carefully thought out. Seekers and Christians alike were provided with opportunities to share stories of emerging faith. These narratives were often used to point out the leading of God in their lives. Seekers were seeking, they were told, because of

God's prevenient work in their lives through the Spirit; it was providence, not coincidence, that brought them to this point. In this way they were exhorted to begin the pilgrimage of faith in earnest, and the spiritual practices and disciplines such as praying, fasting, repentance and forgiveness probably began at this point. They shared worship in the group, but not yet public worship with believers. This first phase – technically termed the 'pre-catechumenate' – often ended with a special ritualized event, giving the opportunity for people to continue or withdraw with dignity.

Growing catechumens

Next was a lengthy process of further enquiry and instruction. We must not put post-Enlightenment heads on pre-enlightenment shoulders, but it is clear that there was more to catechesis than being taught doctrine. Yes, they were taught the faith; yes, they did read and have expounded the Scriptures; yes, the role of the catechist was vital, but notions of third-century boring Confirmation classes must be dispelled! There appears to have been an emphasis on experience and encounter, of turning from evil and holding fast to God in Christ. There was discovery and dialogue, prayer and purgation, openness and obedience. There was rite and ritual, rote and rigour. It was as if the whole person – soul, mind and body – was being engaged. Through this came the repeated invitation to believe and this meant commitment to Christ, his people the Church, the imitation of his lifestyle and the taking up of the life of faith.

Preparing the 'Elect'

At a certain point in the process the mood moved from exploration to preparation. The catechumens began to be referred to as the 'Elect' and spiritual preparation for serious Christian commitment ritualized and sealed supremely in baptism began in a new and serious way. Prayer, fasting and ritual exorcisms increased (often over the period of Lent) ending in a joyful, serious, 'public' baptism when, for the first time, the believer took his or her place in the congregation of the faithful and shared fully in corporate worship, including Holy Communion.

Developing disciples

Many models of catechesis stopped at baptism, but some didn't. These outline a continuing context of sharing and teaching (known as 'post' or 'mystagogical' catechesis). It is at this point that further integration into the main congregation took place – throughout Christian history the transition of believers from small, intimate groupings into larger congregations has entailed sensitivity and skill. At this point the believers would be encouraged to exercise the gifting and talents identified and sanctified through the catechetical process, for the good of the Church. It was at this point also that, for the first time, the baptized believers were referred to as 'disciples'.[15]

Catechesis – why is it so important today?

Some readers will have found this account of historic catechesis interesting in its own right. Others will not! 'What has all this got to do with making disciples now, in the twenty-first century?' they will ask.

A good question, to which I believe there are several good answers:

- *It is a tool for post-Christendom . . . as it was for pre-Christendom.*

Catechesis appears to be a chosen – even anointed – tool for making Christian disciples *in a time of cultural transition*. It was at its most useful and effective in the context of 'in-betweenness', a period when the Church was moving from the margins of Roman society – weak, misunderstood, sometimes despised – towards a place near the heart of Roman society – powerful, influential and respected. Put more technically, catechesis was a profoundly influential instrument for evangelism, conversion, nurture and discipling during the transition from pre-Christendom to the origins of Christendom.[16]

It has been a recurring theme of this book that we are exiting the Christendom enterprise and entering a post-Christendom context, with many ramifications for the Church. Post-Christendom is in many respects worlds apart from pre-Christendom and simple equations about vastly different environments are foolhardy. Equally foolish is the notion that Christians living prior to the age of Christendom have nothing at all to teach Christians like us, living in its aftermath. I consider that this ancient method of disciple-making embodies holistic principles and resonances deeply relevant to our own needs today and is ripe for reappropriation. I believe its time has come again.

- *Catechesis made disciples in religiously plural contexts.*

After centuries of assumptions about 'Christian Europe' and 'Christian Britain' – itself the language of Christendom – the present and increasing religious and cultural plurality of the West is regarded by some as a fall from grace. Perhaps it is. It is salutary to realize, however, that the Early Church lived naturally in a context of great plurality. Catechesis operated effectively when Christianity did not have a religious monopoly, or the assumed faith default position. Catechesis was the means whereby people became disciples as they lived cheek-by-jowl with people of all sorts of faiths and belief systems.

This religiously plural context not only included some 'formal religions' – the equivalents of Islam and Hinduism today – but also, importantly, 'implicit' religious systems – the close equivalents of New Age and New Paganism today. I recall the impact *The Faith of the Unbeliever* made upon me when I read it in the mid 1990s. It was this book that first convinced me of not only the slow demise of Christendom Christianity, but also of the related need to take seriously the pervasive nature of 'unbelief' that largely filled the gap. Unbelief was not non-belief. Rather, an 'unbeliever is not someone who does not believe in God' but one 'who has chosen to step outside of the Christian tradition either to express an informal faith or to celebrate having no particular religious faith'.[17] The notion of Christian Britain was blown apart. The persistent folklore that if the Church got its act together, made worship more relevant, played the right music, heated the sanctuary, ripped out the pews and the like, then hordes of folk would gratefully return to church was rejected for the myth it is. Instead, the 'unbelievers' of Britain need to engage with strategies for mission and witness as robust and thought-through as those for any other faith system. Traditional (Christendom) models of evangelism, confirmation training and so on seemed increasingly unrelated to such a situation. Catechesis, as the means whereby Christian disciples were made in a religiously plural environment not unlike our own in the West today, took on new possibilities and potentials.

- *Catechesis worked effectively in situations when there was very little Christian knowledge, experience and 'churchedness' to draw upon.*

The context outlined above meant that catechesis took place in an environment in which few people had any real knowledge or experience of the Christian faith or had quirky or inadequate impressions of it. It assumed very little about seekers other than that they were seeking. When preparing for baptism, the catechist asked the candidates something like this: 'When you first sought the Way you did not know what you sought. You did not know the light of Christ, the truth of God, the illumination of the Spirit. Now you do. You have been taught it, experienced it and invited to live in it. Now I ask you, do you want to become a Christian, a disciple of the Lord Jesus Christ?'

Contrast this with (Christendom) assumptions about commitment and belief. Someone turns up for worship three weeks running and in a month they are a property steward! Why? Because we readily assume they are 'returning' to faith. But this is not the case now. Now in the majority of cases, we would be calling people to return to nothing. Catechesis, therefore, starting further back, assuming very little, taking longer, going deeper is a better process of making disciples in our increasingly post-Christendom culture.

- *Catechesis worked well in a variety of contexts and among different sorts of people.*

We tend to assume that the Early Church was homogeneous, all the same. It wasn't. Christianity in Africa, Syria, Rome or Jerusalem was quite different. Catechetical processes seemed to have worked successfully in these quite different places. In the fourth century 'full-blown' systems of catechesis were developed by Cyril of Jerusalem and Ambrose of Milan – East and West and, in significant respects, different worlds. Yet authentic Christian disciples were made in both contexts through the processes of catechesis which, while certainly orthodox and classically Christian, also reflected the different cultures and needs of the candidates in both places, and as such were quite dissimilar at various points. It is also worth noting that besides being found in a wide variety of places, catechesis enabled disciples to be created among the rich and poor, educated and uneducated, slaves and free, the somebodies and the nobodies. Christians were made in cities and in villages, in settled times and periods of persecution, among men and women and young and old. Catechesis, it appears, was just what is so desperately required today, a robust, orthodox, transferable and contextual means of making Christian disciples among a 'rainbow' population of different ages, stages and phases.

- *Catechesis worked because it was holistic and multifaceted.*

At least since the Enlightenment – the age of reason, beginning in earnest in the late seventeenth century – what it means to 'believe' and profess Christian faith has gone through a process of reduction.[18] Not a reduction as in cooking, where the flavour of the sauce gets stronger, more a reduction in terms of dilution, where something gets weaker and less distinct. The result is that Christian belief for many consists of nothing more than a series of mental assents to various doctrinal statements. This mentality permits the understandable but essentially inadequate practice of leading those who respond to evangelistic appeals through a few 'spiritual laws' then, when assent to these is given, declaring the convert to be a Christian. The mindset of modernist Christianity has been essentially cerebral.

Catechesis stands in sharp contrast to this reductionist view of believing. The whole person was involved, not just their head. All the senses were engaged. There was passivity and reception, decision and action. A healthy balance between believing, belonging and behaving was attempted because in catechesis they were all of a piece; each signalled the authenticity of the others. The equally important balance between individualism and corporate identity, between personal freedom and social responsibilities is evident in catechetical processes. It included opportunities for self-reflection, decision-making and decision-marking, personal development, chosen obedience and instruction. In a sentence, catechesis took whole human beings wholly seriously, their complexities, grandeur and sinfulness, potential and pitfalls. Above all there was an explicit reliance on the work of the Holy Spirit, without whose presence and infilling, through convicting, converting, enabling and accompanying all else was regarded folly.

• *Catechesis worked well because it took time.*

The evocative phrase used by ancient catechists to describe the process they facilitated is 'from darkness to light'. When reading their accounts of catechesis the crude image of someone being 'cleaned out' comes to mind! It is as if the process engages the darkness of paganism, sucks a little of it out, then fills the space with the light of the gospel through rituals of cleansing and freeing. This process, repeated over time, and culminating in baptism and Communion, brought a person ritually and spiritually from darkness to light. This clearly took time and in our I-want-it-all-and-I-want-it-now society this stands as a salutary lesson that good things cannot all come quickly. Both would-be disciples and the churches that disciple them will have to revise the time, effort and sacrifice involved.

In recent years I have become an Emmaus Road person as much as a Damascus Road one. I think it normally takes time for humans to become Christians. I do not doubt that God can and does 'zap' human beings, I've been zapped a time or two myself! But equally I have little doubt that becoming a Christian is a journey, like the Emmaus story, with its evocative imagery of taking from morning till night. It is not that conversion is *either* 'crisis' *or* 'process', it is that conversion *is* a process in which there *are* points of crisis. The whole makes for discipleship. The mistake of much evangelism is not that it stresses the significance of being 'born again' but that it equates such vital points of crisis with the complete nature of Christian conversion and discipleship.[19]

I suggest it takes about three years, at least, to get to grips with becoming a Christian. Some would say much longer. Catechists such as Tertullian, Cyril and Ambrose knew this. The full-blown process of discipling they outline takes about three years.

Some years ago John Finney interviewed about 500 people who had recently professed Christian faith in some public way. He observed that, on average, it took between three to four years from a person's initial personal interest in Christian faith to the point of formal profession of Christian faith.[20] If Finney relayed how to open the front door of the church a little wider, Philip Richter and Leslie Francis related how the back door of the church might be closed a little firmer. Their research into why people leave church today suggested that people did not wake up on a Tuesday morning and declare to the world 'I'm giving up church!' Rather, people went through a process of 'deconversion' which, though no firm time-scale was given, suggested a small number of years from the point of initial disaffection to completely severing the ties which once bound.[21] It seems that it takes humans some time to truly 'change their minds'. Faith development theorists have long known this. They suggest we humans move through faith stages throughout our lives. We do not all move at the same speed, or in the same direction, but many experts are agreed that for a person to make a decision to change, at a profound level, takes a period like three to four years.[22]

One is led inevitably to the conclusion that some two millennia ago the supreme catechist, a young Jewish Rabbi, who gathered 12 disciples round him and trained and mentored them for about three years, knew exactly what he was doing!

Catechesis – premodern discipling for postmodern disciples

Catechesis gave full attention to discipleship. Its primary aim was a holistic and healthy experience that included seeking, repentance, forgiveness, conversion, salvation, liberation, teaching, cleansing, committing, believing, belonging, behaving, renewal, infilling, refilling. Such is needed today. Through *Alpha*, *Emmaus*, *Disciple*, *RCIA*, *Essence* and the like we are beginning to see the beginnings of catechesis and its possibilities. However, more is needed if authentic disciples are to be made in our present post-Christendom context, with its heady mixture of challenge and potential. A thorough revisiting, appropriate revision and innovative implementation of catechesis may be God's anointed tool for discipleship once again. The recovery of tools for enabling authentic disciples of Jesus Christ to be made today is a crucial aspect of renewal today.

To mull over . . .

- Think of the people who introduced you to Christian faith and describe their characters. Did their words match their actions?

- Reflecting upon the process of catechesis, what beliefs or practices are essential for becoming mature disciples of Jesus? Try to produce an outline of what should be involved in a catechesis programme.

9

Renewing Ministry

Vocation is finding a purpose for being in the
world that is related to the purposes of God.[1]

Walter Brueggemann

Challenging Cuba

In late 2005 I spent some time in Cuba. The Methodist Church in Cuba is experiencing significant revival,
and it was marvellous to be with Christians so vital
and passionate about their faith and to participate in
the kind of inspired meetings that most only read or
dream about. Their recent story is wonderful and I
retell some of it here, as it sets out some of the themes
that rumble throughout this chapter.

In the months after Fidel Castro came to power
in 1959 many things changed in Cuba. Two changes
particularly affected the life of the Methodist Church
there. The first was that all the buildings were confis-
cated, technically becoming the property of the state.
In humble churches in the countryside this made little
practical difference, but some of the grander, colonial
church properties in Havana, Santa Clara and in other
cities were actually taken from the congregations
and 'put to good use'. I preached in one such building shortly after it had been returned to the Church.
Once fine and regal, it would have been condemned

as dangerous by British authorities after 40 years of being used as a storage depot by the authorities. The second change was that around three-quarters of the ordained ministers caught a boat or plane and left Cuba, most making the short but significant journey to Florida. By the early 1960s then, the Cuban Methodist Church had no properties to call its own and virtually no clergy to lead it.

What happened over the next three decades or so is best recounted by stories. Many gave up going to church as the prevailing atheistic political climate removed the need for nominal Christians to persist in the practice. Cuban Methodism became lay-led, mostly meeting in homes where family living space doubled as a sanctuary. To my knowledge no formal records were kept and therefore one can only guess how many met in this way, possibly as few as 2,000 or 3,000 – this on an island over 800 miles long. By the 1990s, so the stories go, the lay leaders (both men and women – Cuba's political philosophy has produced an egalitarian view of both sexes as simply 'workers') began to pray earnestly about the future. They were getting old and tired. The Lord must either prepare them for death or renew them.

Slowly, but discernibly, the leaders began to be approached by young couples, often with infant children. The couples wanted to talk. They were content with the political regime and proud of Cuba, but they had questions. 'If it is *society* alone that matters, then why do we feel so committed to *family*?' they asked (Cuba has one of the highest divorce rates in the world). 'If there is no God, then why do we feel these longings to believe there is?' they asked. 'You've come to the right place' said the lay leaders, and they befriended them and led them into the Christian faith and its family.

Two important things then happened. First, the new young Christians were natural evangelists and the church groups began to quickly grow. Second, the old leaders quickly handed on the leadership of these churches and served as mentors to a new generation of lay leaders. Since the mid 1990s the Church has continued to grow in this fashion – and at some pace. During my visit I was proudly taken from place to place where both 'churches' and '*missiones*' flourished. '*Missiones*' are small mission churches planted in the homes of a Christian family as part of a deliberate policy by the sending 'churches' to provide a Christian community in every district or village or street.

The main reason for my visit, however, was not ecclesial sightseeing. I had been invited by the Bishop to help respond to a need. A nice need, of a kind many Christian leaders would love to have. Bishop Ricardo now had hundreds of men and women leading '*missiones*' all over Cuba, mostly untrained, many who felt the call of God to ordination. The lovely, historic, ecumenical theological seminary simply could not cope with the numbers involved and the waiting list was becoming many years long, so he was gathering them together periodically for crash courses in basic training for ministry. In spite of the large numbers of lay pastors, entry into this basic training was not without its demands. The Bishop and others interviewed each person experiencing a call to ordination and it was expected that they could 'demonstrate their call'. This 'demonstration' was effectively the rehearsing or production of a CV, a résumé of the '*missiones*' they had planted thus far, and testimonies from their members about their godly life and effective leadership. They were called to ordained ministry because they could plant and lead churches and nurture Christians, and had done so already.

Often when I tell the story of the Cuban Methodist Church to British congregations or conferences, I conclude, 'So we now know how renewal of the Church will happen: close all your buildings and sack all your ministers!' It is meant to be a joke! Of course, it is silly to suggest that what is happening in Cuba can be exported elsewhere, lock, stock and barrel. On the other hand I believe the Cuban Church has crucial clues for us in relation to the renewal of inherited and transitioning churches in the West. Many of these clues relate to the perceived ministry of the whole people of God, about laity and clergy, about leadership and training. These are the issues with which this chapter mainly deals.

The ministry of the whole people of God

> [The reinstatement of the whole people of God]
> . . . will be realised only if the 'nonclergy' are
> willing to move up, if the 'clergy' are willing to
> move over, and if all of God's people are willing
> to move out.[2]
>
> *Thomas Gillespie*

'The ministry of the whole people of God' has become something of a mantra of western churches in recent times. The phrase is not always properly understood or used. I know of instances when appeals to the 'ministry of the whole people of God' has been variously employed as a way of encouraging greater giving to the church, urging complicity with the minister's latest zany idea, and soliciting more Christian Aid collectors from the ranks of the congregation. More often than not the phrase suggests an ideal to be pursued rather than a reality to be celebrated.

Yet the proper ministry of the whole people of God is crucial if the Christian Church is to become more truly mission-shaped and evangelistically effective. The New Testament conceives a Christian congregation to be a ministering community, rather than a community gathered round a minister. The 'body' language employed to describe the Church of Christ suggests a total and inclusive rather than partial and exclusive ministry. In historical terms the winsome life and vitality of the Early Church sprang from its 'every member ministry'.[3] Indeed, a recurring theme in almost every renewal of the Church in Christian history is a rediscovery of the laity as the quintessential Christian 'ministry'. There appears to be no lasting renewal of the Church without a rediscovery of the ministry of the laity. Indeed 'around the world, churches without paid leadership tend to grow faster than those with paid leadership . . . a less clerically-dependent Church has every chance of being a growing one'.[4] In theological terms it is widely acknowledged that it is baptism, rather than ordination, that provides the essential authorization for Christian ministry, both in the world and in the congregation. In terms of the missionary nature of the Church, too, it is clear that only the releasing of the gifts, energies and skills of the whole people of God will enable large swathes of our culture and society to encounter Christianity in any authentic and meaningful way. Anything less

191

will be insufficient. In short, the claim that the true ministry of the Church is the ministry of the whole people of God seems irresistible.

The emergence of Fresh Expressions and the transition from inherited to mission-shaped church thinking is changing the way in which the ministry of the whole people of God is understood and embodied, though still more change is required. Put simply, mission-shaped thinking is leaving behind many of the inherited understandings and accepted roles of 'laity' and 'clergy' alike, and exploring fresh expressions of 'the ministry of the whole people of God'. A 'new laity' is emerging that requires a 'new clergy', who together form a 'new ministry', an inclusive partnership appropriate for a challenging mission context and consequently embodying a greater possibility of renewal.

A certain kind of laity

New laity and new clergy alike are becoming increasingly critical of inherited understandings of laity which they regard to be predominantly negative and, more importantly, neutering in terms of contemporary mission and ministry. The extent to which lay people have been defined by what they are *not* is both significant and revealing. A negative understanding of laity goes something like this. The *status* of lay people is that they are *not* 'a minister'. The *function* of lay people is that they do *not* administer sacraments. The *education* of lay people is that they are *not* theologically trained. The general *description* of lay people is that they are *not* full-time or paid. The *location* of lay people is *not* in the church but in the world and consequently their *lifestyle* is *not* religious but secular. This is overstated to be sure, but nevertheless the long-term effect of such understandings is that lay people got to know their place in the shape of things and learned to exercise their received ministry as second-class Christians within it.

A certain kind of ministry

Of course the 'first-class Christians' in relation to whom second-class Christian lay people were implicitly defined were the clergy. Here was located ordination, the administering of sacraments, theological expertise, the full-time, paid, religious lifestyle. Here was 'proper Christian ministry'.

Permit me, please, a little more oversimplification to make the point! The traditional clergy(man) was trained to exercise a strong, patriarchal form of leadership. He was the expert among amateurs in all the things that mattered, that is, the life and ministry of the church. He spoke, others listened. He was 'in charge' of the church. He led; others were expected to follow. He spoke for the local church congregation, and represented them and their views in public. He cared for his 'flock'. He comforted them in times of need, and challenged them to what he considered an acceptable form of discipleship. He encouraged and managed the routine life of the church. If the basic business of 'being church' was undertaken competently, then he was performing his duties well. A content congregation meant a good minister.

A certain kind of congregation

For their part, the congregation came to value and evaluate their clergy by the clergy's own criteria. A long succession of ministers, quite different, but essentially variations on this basic ministerial model resulted in the congregation coming to assume and accept that such a model *was* ministerial leadership. This was what ministers were and what they did. The congregation knew what to expect. A minister was supposed to be educated, so he was expected to be clever and erudite. The congregation had been taught to appreciate 'good sermons', so they complained at 'bad' ones. They expected their minister to be a good pastor and visitor and he was judged hard if he did not measure up in this respect. If he didn't take a lead in the way it was thought he should, he was either not doing his job, or was poorly trained, or was simply a poor minister. He had his work to do, and they supported him in it. They were a team. He taught them what it meant to be a good congregation, one that enhanced his own understanding of ministry, which in turn reinforced the received notion of the proper relationship between a 'good' clergyman and a 'good' laity.

A lasting legacy

This model of the 'ministry of the whole people of God' persists today in many churches, in spite of hopeful signs of rebellion. A survey taken some years ago among several thousand American Methodist lay people illustrates this point. Participants were asked to choose one option from the following list that best described their understanding. Lay people are:

- members of the people of God called to a total ministry of witness and service in the world

- people who are ministered to by the clergy who are the true church

- people in part-time Christian service

- non-ordained Christians whose function is to help the clergy do the work of the church.

Almost 60 per cent chose the last option![5] Similarly, when commenting about the results of a questionnaire circulated among local churches about their expectations of ordained ministers, a recent report stated:

> The main aim . . . seems to be to maintain a certain number of ministers. Nothing about worship and mission. Not even the suggestion that the people need ministers to help them as they engage in worship and mission. When asked what sort of ministers they want they tend to say 'An All-Rounder.' They seem to think that the people exist to maintain the ministers, and the ministers just exist to do everything for the people. It's as if the minister is a sort of Church butler, who ensures that all the household jobs get done and that everyone's need is catered for, whilst the Church Family take their leisure or indulge in whatever takes their fancy.[6]

A dependency culture of disempowerment

My aged parents and parents-in-law are, as so many of their generation and those just now entering retirement, intelligent, gracious, somewhat deferential

195

lifelong Christian churchgoers. They largely take their place among this kind of congregation in the sense that their perception of their role as lay people and that of 'the ministry' is largely shaped by this understanding. And no wonder. For as long as they can remember this has been the mutually accepted arrangement. It has, in truth, provided for them enormous wells of blessing, comfort and inspiration, and has, in turn, received from them great investments of commitment, time and money.

Yet even among such good folk there are the murmurings of discontent. It takes two different forms. The first is discontent when the 'arrangement' doesn't work well. When, for example, the minister is deemed lazy, incompetent or fails to fulfil the expected role, or when nobody can be found to take over a 'job in the church' that they have done loyally for many years, leading to charges that some members are not pulling their weight. In both examples one or other party is not sticking to the 'arrangement'. The second form is a deeper discontent, a rumbling disquiet stemming from the realization that the life of the local church has become synonymous with the life of faith but in fact can no longer sustain it adequately. It is manifest in the heart-rending awareness that the 'arrangement', which largely constitutes their own Christian 'diet' down the years, seems unable to attract, engage or keep huge numbers of their children and grandchildren. It is then that these chronologically older groupings in the church begin to question the 'arrangement' itself. This questioning gives rise to many of the themes touched upon in this book, about the priority of people, the place of property, the need for renewal, transitioning, fresh expressions of church and the requirement for appropriate evangelism. The 'arrangement' comes to be regarded increasingly, even by some profoundly shaped by it, as mutually disempowering, producing neither a laity nor a clergy shaped for effective mission and ministry today. Whether they articulate it explicitly or not, more and more Christians in the West today are coming to realize that the inherited model of the ministry of the whole people of God has produced a dependency culture, resulting in a Church too often living in its own little world, rather than being enabled and freed to take its rightful place in the mission of God. This realization is a key reason for an upsurge in mission-shaped church thinking today, and the increasingly urgent quest for other models of ministry and leadership.

Towards a better understanding of the ministry of the whole people of God

It is important at this point to make clear that I am not taking sides or allotting blame. Nor am I setting up a 'laity good, clergy bad' Orwellian dualism. Still less am I advocating that all Christians should exercise the same ministries. What I am stating is that a mixture of certain understandings of ministerial leadership and certain understandings of laity have combined together to produce a neutered version of the 'ministry of the whole people of God', which has little going for it biblically, theologically, historically or missiologically. Not surprisingly, therefore, it is recognized to be past its sell-by date by increasing numbers of both laity and clergy, particularly those who are adopting fresh expressions of the ministry of the whole people of God.

197

Including the exclusion zone

One crucial aspect of fresh expressions of ministry is an emphasis upon wider *participation*. This is expressed in various ways. For example, some point out that the older models of laity and clergy effectively excluded laity from the ministry of the church in any meaningful sense, which they regard an injustice that needs to be put right.

> It is time to begin using inclusive language when referring to ministry. In fact, the unbiblical use of the terms 'ministry' and 'laity' is the most extensive and oppressive form of exclusive language in the church. When we use gender-exclusive language, we exclude about 50 percent of all Christians. But when we use the minister/layman (sic) distinction, we exclude 90 or 95 percent of all Christians! It is time to be truly inclusive by referring to all Christians as ministers and banning the term 'layman' (sic) whenever it means Christians who are not ministers.[7]

This represents nothing less than the 'abolition of the laity'[8] as a category of Christian, replaced by the owned conviction that every Christian is a minister. Of course, simply changing its name does not alter the nature of a thing, but it is often a crucial step in beginning to clarify misunderstanding. It seems particularly the case that those engaged in fresh expressions of church tend to think of themselves as 'in ministry' rather than 'merely' lay people, in the sense that they are participating in the mission of God and the ministry of Christ through God's commissioned and anointed vessel, the Church.

It is still possible, however, for Christians to 'abolish the laity' and take up their ministry, which is understood as the old kind of laity! It is important to note, therefore, that the increasing commitment to wider participation more often challenges models of traditional laity than it accommodates them. Let me reintroduce my forty-something friends and some twenty-something Christians, like my sons, at this point. At least a generation apart, both groups are clear that being a Christian means participating in the Christian church in a different way from that of my parents' generation. One friend I know plays a mean guitar. After he was converted he warily made his way to his local church and left it again quite quickly. Fortunately he was encouraged by friends to try another church in the locality and remains there still. The crucial difference is that in the church he made home he plays guitar in the worship band. One student congregation expresses its commitment to the down-and-outs living by the railway sidings by maintaining a long-term rota so that at any time three members live among them, cooking meals and providing some basic hygiene. For these and for many others, commitment, discipleship and 'ownership' in the sense of belonging, is expressed through participation. Without authentic participation there is much less chance of commitment, discipleship and belonging. The traditional role of the laity was, to use a phrase of another friend, 'Turn up. Pay up. Shut up.' New laity is more about active participation than passive observance. That, for very many today, is how you express and live out your faith.

We should not be surprised at this, as it mirrors a significant change in the way most of us in the West under about 50 years old were taught to learn. My parents (who left school at 14) sat in straight rows and copied onto paper in black ink what the teacher wrote on the board in white chalk. They recited things over and over again. When my children went to primary school they sat round tables in groups and made regular sorties to the paint, crayons, clay and reading corner. In important respects new laity *are* quite different kinds of people to old laity. The infamous Baby Boomers are themselves now well into middle age and naturally bring some 'Boomer' traits into their Christianity. Unlike most of their parents they are anti-institutional; loyalty and commitment come not so much through historic ties or identities as through networks and friendships, through participation and a sense of ownership. They more naturally adopt a 'flight from deference' talked about by sociologists and cultural commentators. They remain intrinsically suspicious about hierarchies and authority (even though many of them now hold reins of power and influence). Consequently they tend to get impatient with unwieldy or inflexible organizations, particularly if they appear not to listen, or prevent participation. They prefer a practical approach, and if they cannot exercise head, heart and 'hand' involvement they tend not to get involved at all.[9]

A 'thin' place

This active participation traverses the traditional boundaries of 'church' and 'world', where the clergy ran the church and the laity lived in the world. Of course, lay people have always 'done things in church'. My mother has arranged more flowers in church than there are in Kew Gardens! Children read lessons, youths did dramas, and mothers and daughters lit candles. And thank goodness they did – and do. New laity, however, feels the need to enter 'deeper' into church. Making tea if you are a woman and painting window frames if you are a man belongs to a different era of laity in terms of identity and function.

The change is subtle and therefore difficult to put succinctly, but is nonetheless profound and has something to do with how the relationship between the church and the 'world' is experienced. Whether intentionally or not, the older 'arrangement' implied that you somehow left the world when you entered the church, and your life in church fuelled you to return to the world. It was as if Christians lived underwater all week holding their breath, then gulped in air during each visit to church for worship or fellowship before returning to the deep. The most common type of prayer by vestry stewards I have experienced in over 30 years of itinerant preaching have followed the 'Thank you, Lord, that we can come away from the clamour of the world to meet with you here in this quiet hour' type. New laity instinctively holds church and world closer together. I recently asked a very smartly dressed young woman who she was and what she did. She gave me a beam and said, 'I'm Jennifer. I'm a disciple of Christ cunningly disguised as a solicitor.' The life of new laity as people, as humans, as Christians, is all of a piece. It is not that what goes on in church is the *same* as the rest of their lives, more that their Christian faith must be integrated into all aspects of their lives. It has to be or it is not real and can't be sustained with integrity. The older models of separating church and the rest of life therefore appear just too schizophrenic.

Rather than reducing the significance of the role of church in the lives of new laity, the Christian community becomes absolutely crucial. This is one reason so many people today cannot live or flourish in churches where old models of church and world, clergy and laity exist. My friends who went to church in their thirties and left it again in their forties felt this issue acutely. Beyond all the usual reasons of backbiting church members and long, ineffective and uninspiring church meetings, fundamentally it was the lack of integration between life in church and . . . well, just life, which proved too much for them. Church did not make enough sense of their lives, and their lives did not make much sense in church. Church was not a sufficiently 'thin' place for them. The walls between the spiritual and the secular were too thick. Heaven and earth were simply not close enough together to sustain Christian discipleship. Participation, for new laity, is more than 'reading the lesson', or even playing guitar in the worship band, though these will continue. More profoundly it is about participating in a faith community where who you are and what you are is offered into its life, and received with rejoicing, in order that you can be a disciple of Christ in every aspect of life. For increasing numbers of people, for a variety of reasons, the older model of laity and clergy, of being church, is unable to create or sustain that crucial function.

A new clergy

> While 'traditional' pastors may do all they can to
> cling to their old authority, a shift is underway
> to a more scriptural model of the local church as
> an incarnation of the Body of Christ.[10]
>   *Richard Kew and Roger White*

What is often referred to as 'clericalism' is a huge
problem for many Christians today, lay and ordained
alike. My earlier description of 'a certain kind of
ministry' may well be a caricature, but is a model
of clerical leadership that is identified by many as a
significant barrier to moving towards a better ministry of the whole people of God. Diarmuid O'Murchu,
a Catholic layperson, provides a particularly vivid
account of this, taking up the themes of exclusion and
participation outlined above. He comments:

> Currently, the Catholic Church universally
> consists of 1.1 billion members, 99 per cent
> of whom are lay people of non-clerical status.
> Yet, anywhere and everywhere I turn, I find
> that church is both defined and activated
> primarily according to the rules and expec-
> tations of its governing clerical body . . .
> it is clericalism that runs and controls the
> Catholic Church. Innate to such clericalism
> is a patriarchal, sub-conscious driving force
> which is much more about power in the
> name of religion, rather than about service
> in the name of spirituality.
>
> As a lay person, I feel I don't belong any
> more in the closed world of clerical domina-
> tion; I am weary of power games, ritualism,
> moralism and all the empty rhetoric. I am
> more interested in egalitarianism, vulnera-

bility, prophetic contestation, engaging with the God of the flesh, the God of passion, the God of real personal, interpersonal and earthly incarnation.[11]

It is easy to dismiss this as the hyperbole of a disgruntled Catholic, and it may well be the case that the model of clericalism he rails against is peculiarly prominent in Catholicism. I suggest, however, that even the 'lowest' Protestant denomination has its own version of clericalism, and that its negative force cannot be dismissed by simple appeal to belonging to a denomination that rants on about the priesthood of all believers.

Feminist writers particularly have been profoundly critical of models of leadership that they regard as masculine orientations of possession, control and authoritarianism. Mary Daly is one such writer. She lists 'Eight Deadly Sins of the Fathers' which can be summarized thus:

- *Processions:* adopted procedures that seem to involve other people but are in fact imposed from on high, so that what looks to be a new and creative way to proceed is in fact yet another version of manipulation and oppression.

- *Professions:* knowledge and expertise deemed to require specialists who, as such, hold the keys and lord it over everyone else.

- *Possession:* the masculine trait to need to be in control, and therefore dictate what is valuable and to be valued, but inevitably at the cost of consigning everything other than what they choose, and everyone else's giftedness, to oblivion.

- *Aggression:* destructive violence perpetuated mainly by men (often against women).

- *Obsession:* whenever persons are made objects.

- *Assimilation:* a 'cultural gluttony' whereby experiences are 'eaten up' and diminished.

- *Elimination:* an envy or jealousy that dismisses the other, causing them to feel as if they don't exist or matter.

- *Fragmentation:* a policy of 'divide and conquer' which undermines initiative and creativity.[12]

Daly's reference to 'Fathers' is not, of course, an explicit reference to priests or clergy. Her main concern is to outline 'masculine orientations' which she sees as deeply destructive to everyone (but particularly women). For our purposes here the 'sins' themselves are more significant than the 'fathers' in the sense that the inherited model of ministry (whether embodied by male or female clergy) seems to resonate with a good deal of Daly's list and is therefore deemed to be dangerous and damaging. Indeed, it is because these 'sins' are significantly discernible in the Church that Christian feminists seek to reform it, while still others reject the Church as it is currently as irredeemable.

Whether feminist or not, many mission-shaped thinkers concur that the patriarchal, clerical model of leadership plays a major part in producing the disempowering, dependent, mission neutering 'arrangement' that must now be left behind. New models of ordained leadership are therefore crucial, just as are models of lay leadership. It is not a question of no leadership or some leadership, but what sort of leadership. Leadership remains absolutely vital today, but leadership appropriate to the context and the people, enabling a reflourishing of the ministry of the whole people of God, which in turn finds its origin, meaning and focus in the mission of God.

Hierarchy and leadership

We must not confuse hierarchy with leadership. The Church of the New Testament was laden with effective leadership but was not heavy with hierarchy. This, John Robinson notes, is surprising given the cultural context of the time: 'One of the most remarkable facts in the history of religion is the astonishing and well-nigh total eclipse in the New Testament of the priestly side of the Old Testament religion . . . The *un*priestly character of early Christianity must surely have been one of the first things to strike an outsider, whether he were Jew or pagan.'[13] Of course, a certain kind of hierarchy became normative in the Church, in both East and West, largely mirroring its cultural context throughout centuries of changing models of Christendom. It is silly to suggest that every aspect of every hierarchy is anathema or unnecessary, or resort to the equally impractical suggestion that all existing hierarchies be immediately abandoned. Leadership, by its very nature, creates some sort of distance and difference. Nonetheless it remains the case that leadership in the present cultural context needs to be less dominated by the hierarchical, patriarchal models of the past, if not by nomenclature then certainly by practice.

Lighter, flexible ad hoc leadership

At this present time we need leadership that better resembles the 'ad hocness' and charismata of the New Testament rather than the regimentation of Rome or the autocracy of Geneva. As Alvin Tofler commented, emerging society will be characterized not by aristocracy, meritocracy or democracy but by ad hoccracy![14] This does not mean anything goes, by anyone who feels like it. Nor does it mean an absence of accountability or authority. There is a wide gap between clerical authoritarianism and charismatic authority, and we need to move further away from the former and closer to the latter. This will require a lighter structure, a lighter touch and a broader understanding and recognition of authority and anointedness. Such a change in direction will help bring about the *flexibility* in ministry that is so crucial today and so full of potential for renewal. The Cuban Church situation illustrates this well. There is structure. There is hierarchy. The pastors are required to be recognized, assessed, authorized and commissioned. They are expected to lead, possess spiritual authority and giftedness, and be accountable to both the bishop and the congregation in respect of their ministry. However, there is a lightness to it all, a deep pragmatism that is governed by the wooing of the missionary God, as if the whole Church is waiting to pick up the breath of the Spirit and immediately trim its sail to travel in the right direction. It is as if the Church has found its reason for being, which is outwards focused, yet, wonderfully, this very pursuit also builds up the Church internally, and its leadership embodies that self-understanding. But remember, the vast majority of such leaders are *lay* leaders. The mission of God, the context and the call to ministry required a new way. The result is energizing, exciting, innovative, flexibility in ministry and mission. It is institutionally messy and renewal-potent, absolutely appropriate, both for them *and,* I suggest, for us in the West.

Intentional flexibility in my own British Methodist context would certainly mean taking with a greater seriousness than ever before two crucial, closely inter-related themes: recognizing God's call to ministry in a *wider variety of people*, and recognizing that the emerging mixed economy of church requires *wider varieties of models of ministry.*

A wider variety of people most certainly includes encouraging *young* leaders – lay and ordained – in their calling. There should be a positive bias to 're-cruiting' young men and women into lay and ordained ministries in the Church. Young leaders relate best to young Christians, and bring naturally apt models of ministry and mission to missing generations in many churches. We have told too many people to 'come back when they are older'. In historic churches where the age profile of candidates for ordained ministries has increased so that the 'average' person is middle-aged with a career and much experience under their belt, we need to consciously relearn how to discern God's call in the life of a contemporary 20-year-old male and female. Equally importantly, having discerned the call, we need to revisit what proper discipling, nurture, mentoring and 'ministerial training' might consist of in order to express and develop the call, rather than assume that they will fit neatly into the existing system of input and outcomes, or go away until they are able to do so. We should not only focus on young adults, however. Our churches must ensure that our selection procedures enable a wide range of different types of people to demonstrate a call from

God and be accepted into training for ministry: people from different ethnic and socio-political groupings; those expressing a variety of learning and behaviour types; those who articulate their faith quite differently from the norms of erudite, educated, 'modern' pedagogy and theological methodologies. Though we may not intend it to be so, very often our present processes of selection result in a far too narrow group of people selected. 'Finding square pegs to fit into our predetermined round holes in order to keep the show on the road is not a good way to unlock the energy and enthusiasm of the square pegs.'[15]

Not surprisingly, fresh expressions of church require fresh expressions of ministry. The ever more various mixed economy of church emerging around us is the challenging, creative context requiring a great variety of people becoming 'ministers'. Alongside 'pastors' must be trained 'leaders in mission'; as well as 'curators' we must train 'planters'; in addition to 'chaplains' we need 'missionaries'; next to 'settlers' we want 'pioneers'. Alongside 'safe pairs of hands' are needed 'risk-takers'; 'managers of decline' need outnumbering with 'inspirers of health and growth', and 'authority figures' with 'authentic adverts'.[16] Above all, we must explode the myth that once trained a lay or ordained minister can go anywhere and do anything. Lifelong learning and specialized ministries go hand in hand in providing vital ministry in the mixed economy.

Strong leadership

The fact that I feel the case for strong leadership requires defending is itself telling. Leander Keck expresses this defensiveness when he comments that many churches and seminaries today take a dim view of 'strong leadership', denigrating it rather than valuing and encouraging it. He continues:

> If the churches are to nourish strong leadership they must be more hospitable to persons with strong egos . . . The impression is abroad that the church does not welcome strength since it is more a place to find a support group than a channel for energy and talent, more a place where the bruised find solace than where the strong find companions and challenge . . . the churches have the opportunity to nurture the kind of persons that society needs to lead its institutions, including the churches themselves.[17]

I believe that one of the great needs of churches today, whether inherited, transitioning and emerging is strong leadership, but I want to explore a little further what I mean by that. Strong leadership is not to be confused with authoritarianism. There are many different ways of being strong. Strong leadership, for example, involves being openly vulnerable. It involves being wrong, together with the ability to acknowledge this fact without fear or defensiveness. It involves a readiness to acknowledge that you do not know – or have – all the answers. It involves trusting people with responsibilities. It involves openness to the gifts of others, and a conviction that God's will comes through many voices and not just yours. It involves receiving help and ministry as well as offering it. It involves the willingness to live in a mess, rather than have things neat and tidy. Strong leadership involves not abusing the power you possess, not wrongly manipulating what you can. It involves not always speaking when you could, not always having the last word. Strong leadership involves being 'human', being 'persons as well as parsons', as Robert Warren puts it about ordained leaders. This involves integrity, authenticity, and a willingness to reveal who you really are. Strong leadership involves Christian spiritual discipline, being committed to 'the means of grace' and the lifestyle of discipleship when you least feel like it. Strong leadership involves following as well as leading: following Christ, following God's call, following the missionary Spirit of God, following in humble obedience. Such is a proper model of strong leadership for today, and it will commend itself in good measure to lifelong members, Baby Boomers, and young zealots alike.

Facilitating leadership

> When the best leader's work is done the people
> will say 'we did it for ourselves'.[18]
>
> *Tony Benn*

Another key difference between new leadership and old clericalism is an open acknowledgement that the clergy must cease to function primarily as 'the deliverers of ministry' and begin to operate as 'an enabling ministers'. Leaders (mainly ordained leaders at this particular point) must change from seeing their role as attempting to do the entire ministry to see it as helping equip the whole Christian community to engage in the mission of God. This liberates the whole church for the ministry that Christ gave it. Providers must become facilitators. When this begins to happen clergy cease to focus on doing things *for* people, do more things *with* people and increasingly enable the whole people of God in their ministry. This is an empowering rather than disempowering style of leadership. It enables rather than disables, encourages rather than daunts.

A growing number of young and middle-aged Christian women and men I know are benefiting hugely from this kind of ministry, some of them in church traditions usually associated with older models of ministerial authoritarianism. A leader/pastor meets regularly with them, sometimes individually, sometimes in small groups, sometimes in a café over lunchtime, and 'mentors' them. They talk openly about every aspect of life and faith, about the 'world the flesh and the devil'. They pray for each other, often there and then. They sometimes make each other accountable, laying down mutual expectations in light of their conversations. From such facilitating leadership I witness both stronger Christian disciples and new leaders emerging. This model of leadership is much better fitted to new laity than old. A few of my friends have 'remained in church' largely because such ministry is offered and received. Nor, in many cases, is it only *the* pastor or minister who undertakes this ministry. Rather, it becomes a model adopted by considerable numbers in the church, with the result that mentoring becomes a normal part of Christian experience and formation. It is also the case, based on my observations as I meet many different Christian groupings, that this style of ministry is especially prevalent in churches that are mission-shaped and mission-focused.

We have already noted one of the great benefits of this kind of ministry, but pause to register how important it is: it is geared not to servicing the church but to enabling discipleship. It desires to deepen faith in, and love for, Jesus Christ, and seems to do so. It facilitates personal and spiritual growth. It aids the striving for authentic, contemporary holiness. It engenders vision and hope and, wonderfully, arising from all this (rather than the other way round), participation in church and very often an explicit commitment to mission-shaped church and evangelism emerge naturally.

Transitional leadership

> Lay and ordained Christian ministers are...
> called to a dual vocation which might be
> described as transitional leadership: to care for
> what is yet also to seek out and bring into being
> something new.[19]
>
> *Steven Croft*

What I have been outlining here represents a significant challenge to many laity and clergy alike. The clergy needs to come to terms with the challenge and potential of new laity, and old laity needs to come to terms with the challenge and potential of new clergy. The 'stalemate' situations, so common in congregations today, occur when predominantly old laity and new clergy find themselves together, or when primarily new laity and old clergy co-exist in a local church. I have repeatedly had all of the following four types of conversation in recent years: the 'new' clergyperson ruefully resigned about her or his old laity congregation who are 'going nowhere'. The 'new laity' exasperated about their 'old clergy' leader who 'holds everything back'. The 'old' clergyperson, belligerent about 'new laity' who threaten to 'upset everyone else' and 'challenge authority'. The 'old laity' bewildered about the aggressiveness of their 'new' clergyperson who 'only does what they want to do'. I have sometimes comically considered inviting them all to Cliff College and locking them all in a room together until they pair themselves off as they choose!

A large number of local churches are in transition with respect to the ministry of the whole people of God, about primary understandings of the ministry of laity and clergy. Consequently, many church —leaders today recognize the need for transitional leadership – that careful balance between caring for what is while seeking out and birthing the new, what Steven Croft calls a 'dual vocation'.

In the 'mixed economy' of inherited, fresh expressions and emerging churches this dual vocation will itself take several forms, some better than others in terms of mission, ministry and renewal. Some church leaders I know flatly refuse to have anything to do with fresh expressions on the basis that their ministry is to 'care for the flock'. They say that as there is no desire to change from inherited models of ministry, worship or mission, their role is to supply what *is* desired and not waste time or effort introducing what isn't. They sometimes use the language of a 'mixed economy' to defend this view of ministry. 'This is what sort of church we are, others are different and together we are a mixed economy.'

Another group of church leaders I encounter respond to the need for transitional ministry by exercising the dual vocation almost entirely alone. They say that as there is nobody else in the congregation who can exercise this dual vocation, then, if it is to happen at all, to any degree, it must be by their own work and effort. The sad reality is that they often split themselves in two and fall down the gap in the middle with burnout and depression. In my experience it is often those leaders who already work hard to service the inherited system faithfully and conscientiously, and then add another new, demanding strand of ministry who are particularly prone to this. I recall a time of sharing at a major conference where chronologically young ministers shared their sense of frustration that the kind of ministries they felt called by God to exercise were being denied them. This denial came not so much through an overt, flat refusal on the part of their church authorities or local members, but by an implied expectation that all aspects of 'caring for what is' had to be undertaken before any other aspects of ministry – 'bringing into being something new' – could be undertaken. One young woman minister commented, 'I am so exhausted doing the normal things of ministry, I haven't the energy to do the things I really feel I am called to and gifted to facilitate.'

A third group of church leaders I meet are those who have embraced the new ministry with some vigour, but at the cost of the maintaining 'what is'. They say that, as this new ministry is where their particular gifts lie, it is clearly evident where their energies must be placed. They are not always able, however, to carry sufficient people with them to create what they seek, and so move on to try new ministries somewhere else, sometimes leaving behind hurt and mess rather than health and maturity. In short, transitional ministry is a complicated calling.

I consider that transitional ministry requires several ministers (lay and ordained) and ministries to work well. A 'dual vocation' is absolutely right, but this must not be vested in each and every individual minister. Some amount of focus in ministry, which goes beyond the expectation that every minister (lay and ordained) is required to be an 'all-rounder', is necessary. Not to enable this is to court further burnout and frustration and to deprive both churches and wider communities of some of our best resources properly employed for God. God is calling people – lay and ordained – to the dual vocation. It is a fantastically exciting time, but each individual minister offers particular ministries within the whole. This requires, as in Cuba, a much more flexible approach to *local* leadership, where lay ministries, both 'pastoral' and 'evangelistic' (though these are not exclusive by any means), operate in each congregation, however small. It also requires careful and competent supervisory leadership, itself of an enabling, mentoring kind, and certainly one operating quite differently from the one-person-band-who-is-all-things-to-all-people models of ministry from the recent past. Of course, not all necessary types of ministry will be found in each local church, but that in itself must be an incentive to strive for a better version of the ministry of the whole people of God, rather than reverting to putting all the eggs in one basket called the ordained minister. Local groupings of churches are seeking and finding contextually apt models of lay and ordained ministries that enable transitional ministry to take place. These must be further encouraged and resourced. In this respect those who hold positions of authority and power in ecclesiastical units like Anglican deaneries and Methodist circuits are hugely significant.

'Pioneer' ministries

> To recover a theology by the whole people of
> God the theological task must be relocated. The
> academy must work with the congregation, the
> home, and the marketplace.[20]
>
> *Paul Stevens*

I read somewhere that in the years preceding a large-scale war the number of boys born compared to girls was proportionately higher per 1,000 live births, as if somehow nature was preparing sadly for what was to come, but also more hopefully for the future coming after that. Whether this is any more than fanciful surmise I don't know, but the notion of some mystical preparing for the future is intriguing. My observations are that people – lay and ordained – are being called by God into a greater variety of ministries today than for a very long time, possibly even as far back as the earliest Christian communities. Each week I meet people who feel called by God not so much into 'the ministry' as into this or that ministry in the church. For them, alongside the important question 'Does this call involve ordination', lies the crucial issue 'Where does this fit in relation to ordained ministry?' For them, on that issue much rests. They often talk about being called to pioneer ministries, a piece of shorthand outlining a number of ministries, but having in common that they do not appear, at least to those experiencing a call to them, to fit easily into the shape of existing ministries. This is critically important and requires immediate investigation and speedy, appropriate responses by all those involved in ministerial formation and financing. There are, no doubt, several perfectly ordinary explanations for this burgeoning interest in pioneer ministries, but I like to think that God is preparing the Church for what is to come, for renewal. The future is a time when a much greater variety of lay and ordained ministries than we currently affirm, utilize and employ are required, in order to participate obediently and effectively in God's mission.

Our churches have long trained people for 'a certain kind of ministry'. There are many fine exponents of this kind of ministry and they are a great blessing to a mixed economy that will continue to require such ministry for the foreseeable future. Nevertheless they do tend to continue to monopolize all the many kinds of resources denominations pour into training for ministry. As signalled earlier I suggest that there is an increasingly urgent need to identify, affirm, form, equip, resource, bless, commission, deploy and, as necessary, ordain people for other kinds of ministry. Otherwise inadequate resourcing will hamper the desired mixed economy and its required transitional and pioneering ministries. Put starkly, we will be training too many people for yesterday's Church and too few for tomorrow's.

It is a repeated lesson of Christian history that, after a time of renewal or the emergence of a new religious movement, decline sets in. One recognized reason for this is the arrival of a 'settled clergy' whose self-perceived role becomes the maintaining of institutional patterns and who create a general understanding that formal religion is dispensed by the clergy and received by the laity. Alongside this is a recognized corresponding move away from intentional evangelistic, missionary activity. This move brings about its own slow downfall. It is this very reality that propels the need for fresh expressions of church ready to participate in God's mission.

The changes in Cuba came about because of what happened *to* the Church. It is doubtful they would have chosen voluntarily to walk the road enforced upon them. As their pastors boarded boats and planes those remaining must have felt as if it was Good Friday. It is easy, too, to forget that the first signs of new life came not three days but over 30 years later. In between were years and years of small faithfulness, hanging on and praying for a way ahead. The western Church faces an arguably harder task still. It must choose to continue to go down a similar route, with respect to changes to its understandings and practices of laity and clergy alike, rather than have such come through sudden regime change. Leadership and ministry today, and increasingly tomorrow, require a renewed understanding and application of the ministry of the whole people of God. When that comes about, a potent resource for the renewal of both the Church and our society will be released.

To mull over . . .

- 'The Cuban Church has crucial clues for us in relation to the renewal of inherited and transitioning churches'. What do you think these are and what do you think about them?

- To what extent do you recognize the 'certain kind of laity', 'ministry' and 'congregation' outlined in this chapter? What do you make of the assertion that this has produced a disempowering dependency culture?

- What might the 'abolition of the laity' mean in your local church and in your own discipleship of Jesus Christ?

- Do you think the walls between your church and 'the world' are too 'thick' or too 'thin' or just right? Discuss.

- To what extent does your life in church enable your Christian faith to be integrated into the whole of your life? If the answer is 'not enough', for you or others, what might be done about that?

- What kind of leadership do you think your church needs today? What does your preferred model of leader do and not do? What does such leadership 'feel' like?

- What kind of transitional and pioneering ministries do you think are necessary in order for your church to continue to engage in the mission of God in your local neighbourhoods? How might these come about? Is there a commitment to ensure they come about?

10

Modelling Church Renewal

All true things must change and only that which
changes remains true. Everything ages and needs
transformation and renewal.[1]

Carl Jung

The God of mission is constantly seeking to renew the
Church in order that it might share in God's mission
more obediently and effectively. A mission-shaped
church, therefore, for its part, needs to be constantly
open to the renewal of God and attuned and atten-
tive to the ways in which that renewal might come
about.

At the end of the twentieth century an organization
owning and running a number of orphanages met to
consider its future. Founded in the mid-nineteenth
century it now felt itself to be in a state of crisis. En-
dowments were down and income was low. Properties were in need of repair and upgrade. It was getting
ever harder to employ and retain good-quality staff.
So they met together to ascertain if their organization had run its course. Had the days of orphanages
passed? Was its work finished?

The open meeting was traumatic. Benefactors
threatened to withdraw future support unless things

stayed essentially as they were. Balance sheets were produced as evidence that this could not happen. Staff made passionate speeches about the consequences of losing their jobs. Supporters wondered what would happen to needy children. Grandees argued that they were betraying the vision of the founders. There was anger, anguish and tears.

Then, at a certain point in the meeting someone asked how the whole thing had started. Did anyone know? A historian of the organization proudly provided the answer. 'We were founded,' she said, 'to protect and nurture children whose parents or guardians were unable, incapable or unwilling to care for them.' Almost as a revelation it began to dawn on the meeting that building and running orphanages was not, actually, their reason for being, but was itself an *expression* of their core purpose. Excitedly they began to discern again their 'deeper calling' and this rediscovery of their core identity and purpose enabled them to see that their vocation was neither over nor irrelevant.

The cost was enormous, in a variety of ways. Over a number of years they sold off properties given by and named after donors and bought new ones. Fund-raising traditions came to an end and new ones started. The input of hundreds of volunteers finished. Staff were made redundant and others employed in different roles. Children were moved into other settings. Battles with pressure groups opposed to new developments rumbled on. It felt like death. But today, in major cities on the Eastern seaboard of the United States, is a string of child and youth centres with professional drug, sexual health and housing counselling facilities. Death and resurrection. Non-identical reproduction, as the seed of identity and purpose, came to new soil and sprouted into a new organism, the same fundamental vocation by quite different means.[2]

Lessons from Vatican II

Ecclesia semper reformanda (a Church always needs to be reformed)

The Catholic material on renewal I draw upon here first came to my notice through conversation with Dr George Lovell some years ago. George characteristically kept his promise and sent me the papers. I read them and was hooked.

As part of seeking renewal in every part of the Roman Catholic Church, the Second Vatican Council (1962–65) sought to renew the life of its religious orders. A 'think tank' went away and thought and in 1965 *Perfectae Caritatis* – a 'Decree on the Sensitive Renewal of Religious Life' – was published. It outlined five principles:

(a) religious life is essentially about following Jesus

(b) each form of religious life has its distinctive spirit and tradition, which derives from its founder

(c) all religious foundations are to enter into the life of the broader Church and to promote the Church's initiatives

(d) current needs and insights are to be discerned enthusiastically for the sake of the mission

(e) spiritual renewal is a priority in renewing religious life.[3]

These principles were used to review religious orders and over time became summarized as follows:

(a) return to the gospel

(b) return to the founding 'charisms' or 'intentions' of the founder(s)

(c) read the signs of the times.[4]

Taken together, encouraging each to speak to the others in constant dialogue, I have come to regard these as powerful primers, themes for resourcing renewal that enable increased openness to God and therefore facilitate a greater possibility of renewal in the Church, for the sake of the world.

Returning to the gospel . . .

A phrase like 'return to the gospel' is ripe for being misunderstood and it is therefore important to make clearer what is intended by it. The first of the original, longer list of principles gets to the heart of it. Religious life is essentially about following Jesus; discipleship is key. So this primer is about returning to 'the gospel' rather than 'The Gospels'. It is less about appealing to 'Matthew' or 'Luke' and more about shaping the Christian life and its practices on the teaching and example of Jesus Christ. It is like a 'red letter' Bible where the words of Jesus are emphasized in red print. In this case the words of Jesus are the crucial, potential source for renewal; they are highlighted on the pages. Even more specifically, not *every* word of Jesus has equal significance to each Christian grouping. In each grouping are certain prophetic words and key teachings of Jesus that speak into and resonate with its life, witness and purpose. Consequently, because a *particular* community of Christians are 'returning to the gospel' they will revisit the words of Jesus from within their own history, tradition and identity, and teachings that are 'red letters' for one faith community may not be so for another.

Some time ago I was invited to lead a training day for Salvation Army officers and I took them through these three primers for resourcing renewal. I asked them to identify words of Jesus that were for them a 'loud voice', defining texts. Over a hundred officers split into groups of five or six and spent the next half-hour on the task. The ensuing feedback was a time of surprise and revelation for all present. Each group reported how at first it had simply collected together prominent texts. They said things such as, 'We haven't included any parables; we'd better choose one.' Then, when a speedily created list of texts was formed and they began to think they had completed the task in five minutes, someone in the group said something like, 'These are all important, but are they *all* defining texts? Do they all speak to us at the deepest level? Do they articulate who we *are* under God?' At which point they began to whittle the list down again. As each group shared their final 'shortlist' the whole company became more and more intrigued. The shortlists were virtually identical. Occasionally a group offered some words of Jesus not included by any other but time after time, until it was almost comical, the same handful of texts were identified. For example, every group had chosen Jesus' use of Isaiah's words recorded in Luke: 'The Spirit of the Lord is upon me, because he has anointed me to bring good news to the poor. He has sent me to proclaim release to the captives and recovery of sight to the blind, to let the oppressed go free, to proclaim the year of the Lord's favour.'[5] This was clearly 'gospel' for Salvationists. 'Why is this text so special to you?' I asked. 'Because it reminds us why the Salvation Army came into being at all,' said a major, 'it tells us who we are.' Which is, I think, precisely the intended point of this primer for resourcing renewal.

The founding charisms (or charisms of the founders)

This phrase, too, requires some reflection and explanation. First we note that there are variations on the theme: 'charisms of the founders', 'intentions of the founders', 'founding charisms'. Perhaps aware that *charism* is (at least in the sense it is used here) not a common word for many Protestants, George Lovell, in his notes to me suggested 'intentions of the founders' as an alternative. I prefer to stick with the term *charisms* here and like the (mission-minded friendly) definition offered by Doris Donnelly: '*Charisms* are a special variety of gifts dispensed through the Holy Spirit in Church and world, as needed, for the common good.'[6] By comparison, 'intentions' sounds too much like a thing of human determining rather than gifts of a grace-filled God. So charisms it is.

Who are the founders?

In the Catholic material the phrase 'charisms of the founder' is used most commonly. This poses the stimulating challenge of trying to determine whom the 'founders' whose charisms are discerned to be so significant might be. Presumably this exercise will be relatively straightforward for some Roman Catholic Orders such as Benedictines and Franciscans, but more complicated for many other Christian groupings and denominations. In my own Methodist tradition, for example, the founders could legitimately be several groups of people. They could be the several hundred-strong group who effectively sealed 'Methodist Union' in September 1932, formally joining together several branches of quite different Methodism. The founders could also be the mothers and fathers in faith who planted and established a particular local church or chapel, in my case those people who founded Calver Primitive Methodist Chapel in the 1830s, the small Methodist chapel my wife and I attend. Another group of founders would be those who founded a particular grouping – or, as we Methodists call them, 'Connexions'. So in the case of my local chapel it would possibly be people like Hugh Bourne and William Clowes, leaders of the Primitive Methodist movement in the early nineteenth century. Of course, for many Methodists the founders will be John and Charles Wesley, those great figures of eighteenth-century Christianity: John, with his seemingly in-exhaustible commitment to forming and facilitating Methodist Classes and their Societies; Charles, with his seemingly inexhaustible ability to write hymnody that expressed the heart and soul of the people called Methodist. In some senses the answer to the question 'Who are the founders?' is 'All of them' and probably still others.

What are the charisms?

Possibly because of the complexity of identify-ing founders my preferred term for this particular resource for renewal is 'founding charisms'. It is mainly for semantic reasons. Although I know that founders and their charisms are inextricably linked together I consider that it is the charisms themselves, rather than the founders themselves, which are more significant in terms of spiritual renewal in the Church today. For me, therefore, a more important challenge than identifying founders (as individuals or groups) is to try to identify what the founding charisms of a particular religious grouping might be. Certainly this leads us back to the same founding figures but this time we approach them with a different question. We are not now simply asking 'Who are you?' as if correctly identifying founders is itself crucial for renewal. Rather, we are trying to discern the charisms God gave to these founders and enquire for what divine purposes these charisms were given into the life of a particular Christian grouping.

This itself remains a challenging task. Those who formed Methodist Union in 1932 also agreed a Deed of Union, in which are outlined statements of doctrine, practice and discipline that mark out the Methodist Church. Do such foundational documents enshrine founding charisms? The charisms of local chapel founders are often less known and recognized than those of national figures. Even if it were possible to know them we could be disappointed by what we might learn. After all, the nineteenth century was not renowned for an ecumenical spirit that came to characterize the twentieth, and many a chapel was built, alongside stunning spirituality and generous giving, to outdo local 'competition' which, in Methodism, included other Methodist groupings. However, sometimes the birth story of a particular church or chapel is known and is highly significant for the continuing life and ministry of that Christian community. Certainly the founders of particular Methodist Connexions, well-known and well-documented, put their particular stamp upon 'their' chapels. It is said that 'half of Methodism don't know Wesley ever lived, and the other half don't know he's died!' Yet I suspect the majority of Methodists would tend to associate any special charisms of Methodism with the ministries of John and Charles Wesley. But what these charisms might be is not so obvious as to remove debate and dispute. Their long ministries, their developing faith and opinions over many years, their practical responses to fast-changing situations, their prodigious output of texts and hymnody covering a huge variety of topics, make John and Charles Wesley difficult to wrap up or tie down. Consequently they have been targets for almost anyone who wanted to enlist them as supporters, from high-church sacramentalists[7] to new church renewalists.[8] That said, I believe there are some discernible founding charisms, given by God through the Wesleys, which were both the means by which and the reason for which the Methodist movement was 'raised up'.[9]

It will come as no surprise to readers that my own opinion about founding charisms of Methodism is that evangelism, mission and renewal, all undertaken as expressions of an *engaging evangelicalism,* lies at the heart of its being, its identity and purpose. To truly be what it is Methodism must 'offer Christ' to all, as did its founder John Wesley, described by leading scholars as first and foremost an evangelist.[10] Engaging evangelicalism is evident in the formation of the Methodist classes, bands and societies. Over time, these groupings shaped Methodist ecclesiology and identity and were nurseries for conviction, conversion, nurture, assurance and walking the path of Christian perfection and multiple models of social engagement and holiness. Mission and renewal then, are in the DNA. According to Paul Chilcote:

> The Wesley's believed that God raised them up to resuscitate the church. They were not only called into mission themselves but also were equally committed to helping the church rediscover its true vocation by means of their examples. Their ecclesiology, therefore, was essentially missiological . . . All of their energy was directed toward the empowerment of Christ's faithful disciples in ministry to God's world. Indeed, they all viewed evangelism and mission – the proclamation of God's love in word and deed, in witness and service – as the reason for their existence.[11]

Laceye Warner adds: 'While other denominational traditions often trace their roots to disagreements regarding confessional or theological points, the Wesleyan tradition emerged from an evangelistic and missional imperative.'[12] In this sense 'the early Methodist vision for the Church lay in its very provisionality'[13] as an evangelical order within the Church Catholic. In short, 'mission-shaped church' is in the Methodist bloodstream.

There will be dynamic equivalents of such founding charisms for each Christian denomination and tradition. The key is, in the words of the Catholic material, that 'each form of religious life has its distinctive spirit and tradition which derives from its founder'. Such are the 'founding charisms' and, if these primers are correct, then these charisms have a crucial role to play in resourcing renewal. The task of identifying them might be complex and contentious, but the notion and activity is exciting and energizing, and laden with possibilities for renewal.

Some clues about identifying the nature and purpose of charisms are available and I include them at this point. Using Donnelly's definition of charisms outlined above, some closely related things can be said. First, charisms emerge among people not only in the Church but also outside it, in 'the world'. Gifts of the Spirit are not restricted to – or simply given for – ecclesiastical groupings. Second, charisms emerge in response to human needs. Just as Jesus was usually found among the least likely people, so the Holy Spirit constantly arranges these special gifts among unexpected people, but always in response to the holistic needs of humanity, which includes spiritual needs. Third is the notion that charisms are given for the common good. That is, they are not given primarily for the good of an individual, as some special individualized anointing. In this sense charisms are not private possessions, but given to be given, given to build up others.[14] As John Haughey puts it, 'One of the distinctive traits of charisms is that they are given by the Holy Spirit to some for the sake of others.'[15] Consequently we should expect a *missional* and *evangelical* dimension to charisms, as a clear demonstration that they are such. The retrieving of their charisms by a Christian community is a primer for renewal essentially because it refocuses that community on its missionary calling under God.

The signs of the times

The third primer for resourcing renewal is the instruction to read the signs of the times. As with the other themes this is both complex and challenging. Indeed, some people say they have given up trying to read the signs of the times (and in truth some never started in the first place). 'The times' seem so bewildering, or threatening or negative that they have simply resigned from any active engagement with much of contemporary culture, its shapes and communities. (Though, of course, such opting out *is itself* a response to contemporary culture – albeit a negative one.) In terms of church life this often results in a kind of siege mentality in which the life of the local church – often as it is fondly remembered, rather than as it now actually is – provides haven and security for its established members, who sustain its life for as long as possible. However, the gap between church and the surrounding communities and wider culture grows ever greater. Others take a more 'intellectual' stance, arguing that so profound is the fragmentation and complexity of our 'times' that any 'signs' identified will be reductionist nonsense and therefore less than useless.

I do not hold to these views. While appreciating something of the multilayered complexity of our culture, I believe that certain local, national and global 'signs' are discernible. More importantly, I believe too that the Christian faith speaks into our complex culture rather than opts out of it: it is, by nature, always incarnational and contextual. The signs of the times are not neat, nor coherent in a logical, modernist sense, but neither are they so utterly incoherent as to render all 'readings' and discernment nonsense. In some senses this book is an attempt to respond to some signs of the times in the spirit of the Christian gospel. Our present times offer Christians a mixture of excitement and challenge. Robin Greenwood puts the case nicely: 'I want to argue that this transitional period in which the Church has partly lost its way can be recognised as exciting, liminal and challenging, though difficult and personally risky, requiring deep wells of prayer and reflection. There is a dawning realisation that there is no consolation that it will soon be over and a new stability will take the place of change.'[16] More than this, reading the signs of the times is for Christians an exercise in eschatological hope and is deeply rooted in the scriptural understanding of time as *kairos*. That is, the signs of the times speak of God's action and human response. The gospel is always the basis for interpreting the cultural context for the Christian community. The gospel of Christ is the lens through which each contemporary situation, with its 'mixture of difficulties and potentialities, negative elements and reasons for hope, obstacles and alternatives'[17] is discerned and interpreted. As a synod of Catholic bishops put it, 'We should all scrutinize the signs of the times in this age of renewal and interpret them in the light of the Gospel in order that we may work together in distinguishing between spirits, to see if they come from God.'[18]

It is also probably the case that those who proposed these primers for resourcing renewal did not have in mind the need to read every conceivable 'sign' arising from the present 'times', which is indeed a sure-fire recipe for bewilderment and paralysis. A Christian community attempts to engage with all three primers for renewal simultaneously. Therefore a Christian community that returns to the gospel, and revisits its founding charisms will read the signs of the times from within this context. As a result the signs of the times that are 'read' and responded to will be those which resonate with the renewed apprehension of the identity and purpose of that particular Christian community. While remaining challenging, this becomes eminently more possible.

The instruction to read the signs of the times is therefore not one to be dismissed lightly. In terms of openness to renewal, one of the reasons Christians must continue to read the signs of the times is that our present culture is where the renewed church must live and witness and worship. Crucially, too, reading the signs of the times rescues 'returning to the gospel' and to the 'founding charisms' from being merely a backward-looking longing for a past often regarded as far more desirable than the present is or the future is expected to be. The activity refuses to let a Christian grouping live in the past and impels it to live as a gospel community in the present. It refuses to let previous readings of signs of former times continue to dominate and shape the life of the community. In short, reading the signs of the times propels Christian communities into embracing change, at the leading of the Holy Spirit, and from that emerge possibilities of renewal.

Method

It is these three primers *undertaken together* that produces a greater dynamic for openness to renewal. A chronological approach, addressing the first theme, *then* the second, *then* the third, in some linear process, is not the best way to engage with them. It is better to work at all three together, simultaneously, all mixed up, constantly, even if necessarily, for a time, one primer seems more influential than the others. The whole is greater than the sum of its parts. This is challenging but we need not fear, for the vulnerability and risk necessarily involved in the process is more than matched by the promise of the Holy Spirit moving in the life of the communities of believers to reveal the things of God. The Spirit holds together all things, sorts out wheat from chaff, urges renewal and releases wonderful potential for it to happen. But to experience such renewal requires engaging seriously in the task.

Reflecting on the model: identity, purpose and mission context

> Because the ultimate reality in the Bible is personal, we are brought into conformity with this reality not by the two-step process of theory and practice, vision and action, but by a single action comprised of hearing, believing and obeying.[19]
>
> *Lesslie Newbigin*

We are now at the point where a summary of this model for renewal can be made. It suggests that renewal will be more likely to occur within Christian groupings when they engage in a process that involves returning to the words of Jesus that speak particularly to, and roots them in, a gospel tradition, when they re-identify their founding charisms and reconfigure their life and witness around them again, and when they read the signs of the times in order to ascertain how to be the gospel community God calls them to be, here and now.

This Catholic model for renewal, in its own innovative way, suggests that engagement with three fundamental questions is crucial to the potential renewal of Christian communities. The first question is 'Who are we?' the second 'Why are we here?' and the third 'When and where do we live?' The first is a question of *identity*, the second a question of *purpose* and the last a question of *mission context*. These are not quirky, idiosyncratic questions, unique to this material emerging from Vatican II. On the contrary, they are key questions in a good deal of material about renewal, congregational growth and health and mission-mindedness.[20] Put simply, when a Christian community engages seriously with questions of *identity* (who they are under God); with *purpose* (why God raised them up and brought them into being); and *mission context* (what – and how – God wants them to be in the world, here and now), it opens itself to greater possibilities of renewal and thereby becomes intrinsically both more gospel-shaped and mission-shaped.

It is important to recognize that all three of the Vatican II primers contribute to discerning identity, purpose and mission context. Again this works better cumulatively rather than separately. A Christian community does not 'return to the gospel' in order to glean its identity, 'return to the founding charisms' in order to rediscover its purpose and 'read the signs of the times' in order to determine its mission context, in the sense that one produces the other. It is not so clear-cut. Rather it is, by returning to the gospel, the founding charisms and reading the signs of the times, that a Christian community is enabled to glean its identity, rediscover its purpose and determine its mission context. The rest of this chapter explores these interrelated themes and some ramifications of them.

The significance of difference and distinction

Our model for renewal recognizes and accepts difference and distinction in Christian groupings as both a historic fact and a desirable intention for the future.

At a fundamental level each and every Christian church is different and distinct from *the world*. That is why, if it is to be open to renewal and transformation, a Christian grouping must return to the gospel. For it is here that the words of Jesus remind us who – and whose – we really are. It is in returning to the gospel that the challenge is again heard and, if heeded resourced with power, as the Holy Spirit reconfigures a community of Christians to be better disciples of Jesus Christ. The rediscovery of charisms – gifts of the same enabling Holy Spirit – make clear that the church is no ordinary community in the world, but one called to participate in God's mission with a special and specific purpose to fulfil. This awareness of 'who they are' and 'what has been given to them' enables a Christian grouping to interpret the signs of the times in such a way as to locate themselves in relation to 'the world' – locally and globally – as they believe God has made clear. A Christian grouping is reminded that, although it lives in the world and joins the Holy Spirit in loving and wooing and convicting and convincing the world, it is never 'of' the world. It is different and distinct, dancing a different dance to a distinct drum.

Our model for renewal also suggests, however, that every Christian grouping is different and distinct *from each other*, that we are not all the same and God likes it like that. This is not an argument for heresy! The desirability of difference and distinction in this model for renewal does not extend to the fundamental basis of faith – that is why all groupings must return to the same gospel, even if different parts of the teaching of Jesus speak more loudly to different groupings. That is why, though the charisms may be different, they come from the same Spirit. However, within this One Church God raises up each Christian grouping, community, order or family with a distinct identity and endows it with charisms for specific ministries within the whole. Of course, the Vatican II material dealt with different *Catholic* religious Orders and did not countenance this idea beyond Catholicism itself. As such I readily acknowledge I am taking this material to places its originators probably did not intend, but as a mission-minded evangelical Christian I find the idea of distinct identity and purpose exciting and interesting. Earlier material made clear my belief that the missionary God is engaged in the *missio Dei* and constantly inviting humanity to join in. The Christian Church is central and instrumental (though not exhaustive) to the mission of God, through which it finds its true identity, nature and purpose. When the mission of God is unable to proceed with the current human resources available, God does not abandon the mission or remove any human partnership at that point, but raises up new missionary communities that are able to serve as God directs. These are fresh expressions of church in their truest form. Consequently the idea that God brings to birth church traditions, families and groupings with a particular identity and charges them with a particular ministry within the *missio Dei* is not one with which I have a problem! My problem arises when a Christian community seems *not* to know its identity, its purpose and its mission context, when it has amnesia about who it is and about why God brought it into being. Indeed, it is because this model of renewal addresses these very issues and points a way forward that I consider it so important.

Is an emphasis on difference and distinction between Christian groupings anti-ecumenical? For better models of ecumenism I believe not. In fact this model for renewal not only emphasizes the importance of a particular identity and purpose for each Christian grouping, but also clearly locates this within the Christian tradition as a whole. As Romano comments, 'Here we have the deepest reason why every spiritual family must constantly take care that it preserves its own particular spiritual identity, its own original vocation, for these are given for the good of the entire Church.'[21] In missiological terms never before have different and distinct authentic models of organized Christianity been more important. If Christian witness and mission are to become more effective in our post-Christian communities, we need variety. Retaining such authentic, proper difference and distinctiveness within the whole Church is a better way forward than a monochrome Christianity melting into a pseudo-Christian wilderness.

The significance of charisms

Our model for renewal suggests that returning to founding charisms and the renewal of a Christian grouping belong close together. The identity and purpose of a Christian grouping is therefore closely connected to its birth story. This often involves charisms being given by the Holy Spirit to founders, out of whose ministry emerges a religious grouping or community. These charisms, though given to a

239

founder, properly belong to the resulting Christian community, who employ them for others.

The fact that retrieving charisms and renewal belong together should not surprise us. It has often been acknowledged that all communities of people with a core focus or cause move from being a movement to a machine and from a machine to a monument. In the early days of a movement there is excitement, fresh ideas, charismatic leadership, energy, vision, mission. Almost inevitably this changes, sometimes quite quickly, into a more efficient routine. Charismata are ritualized. Convictions are systematized. Means of grace become icons. Energy dissipates. If no fresh impetus reforms or reshapes the institution then it hardens and petrifies into a monument, a sad relic of days gone by. Consequently for a movement to retain its movement it is important to hold nothing sacred except its original calling, its founding charisms.

The attempt to identify and retrieve founding charisms enables a Christian grouping to refocus upon its core purposes, its particular 'calling'. This is a costly but necessary business. Catholic religious Orders undergoing their own reviews discovered that their calling was not 'simply a matter of being busy, but rather, indeed before all else . . . an expression of a definite vocation which is being called today to respond to new situations . . .'.[22] Like many other Christian groupings they discovered that a multitude of laudable roles and functions had built up over time. One Order commented, 'There are a certain number of . . . activities to which the Congregation is committed but where we find our spirit (i.e. charism) only with difficulty.'[23] They became aware of the distance of their current life from their founding charisms.

Their response was to revisit the founding charisms, aware that to 'level off one's own identity, to move away from one's own good, original individuality is, practically speaking, to organize a slow "spiritual suicide". Put simply, it means allowing oneself to dissolve like salt with no savour, alone.'[24] This resulted in a pruning of functions and roles and a refocusing upon the core callings, the founding charisms.

Christian groupings attempting to identify and retrieve their founding charisms face another, equally serious challenge. As one Catholic Order put it, 'There are . . . other activities right in the mainstream of our . . . tradition which are ill adapted to the world and mission of today.'[25] It is one thing to do away with roles and functions discerned not to be your founding charisms, it is quite another to realize that those very charisms no longer seem to fit or enable you to sustain the distinct calling given to you. This will be where many Christian groupings today feel themselves to be. It is a difficult place but a natural consequence of holding together in tension the primacy of founding charisms with a gospel response to the signs of the times.

Some clues that might provide a way forward come from a curious collection of places. For example some biologists, geneticists and social scientists are beginning to write about 'non-identical reproduction'.[26] They write in different ways, but the phrase itself suggests its usefulness here. It talks of something emerging that is not identical to previous versions of itself, but is nevertheless a true reproduction of an earlier species, model or entity. Reproduction is not replication, as the difference between a child and a clone makes clear. Our model for renewal would suggest that, rather than giving up those founding charisms that no longer enable the God-given purpose of the Christian grouping, seeking non-identical reproductions of the charisms is a better way.

We are now able to discern that there are various stages of engagement with founding charisms in a process for renewal. First, there is the *identification* of them – a difficult but necessary and ultimately rewarding undertaking. Next, there is the *retrieving* of them – involving laying down roles and activities that do not marry with them – and refocusing upon them as the central defining characteristics of the grouping. Then, there is the *reproducing* of them – involving the prayerful process of discerning and developing non-identical but authentic versions of founding charisms for today. None of this comes easily, but if the retrieval of charisms is such a fundamental part of the possibility of renewal, it certainly remains worth attempting. The very activity seems to open up possibilities for the Holy Spirit to move afresh and that alone makes the effort worthwhile. And if this is the case, then it is absolutely vital for Christian groupings, denominations, communities and the like to regularly revisit the question 'Why did God raise us up?' Such a question may sound like a hostage to living in the past, but is in fact a key for unlocking a renewed future.

The significance of identity and purpose

Our model for renewal assumes that each Christian grouping, through its engagement with the gospel and the signs of the times, through its birth story and its charisms, has a particular identity. It also assumes that knowing your identity – who you are under God – is crucial to the possibilities for authentic renewal.

In most models of renewal, of various kinds, the birth story is significant. In relation to the life cycles of congregations Alice Mann states, 'These earliest moments in the congregation's story contain powerful bits of genetic information that will express themselves in the rest of the life cycle.'[27] This suggests, using an image becoming increasingly popular in ecclesiology, that not only does the Church have its own DNA,[28] but also that each Christian congregation has its own fingerprint. Eddie Gibbs asserts that each congregation has a distinctive atmosphere and ethos, which arises from factors such as prominent personalities, historical events, its *modus operandi*, value systems, cultural identity and the like.[29] Church congregations then, have identities, and although identities change and develop (and must do), these are defining components in the process of renewal in the sense that a false identity invariably stymies the possibilities of renewal, whereas the rediscovery of true identity and purpose enables renewal. Our model of renewal recognizes, almost instinctively, the significance of identity and its need to be shaped and reshaped by the gospel, by founding charisms and by engaging with the signs of the times.

Reading James Hopewell's book on church congregations[30] was a revelation. I had ploughed through umpteen books about church growth processes and benefited from them, but it was Hopewell who provided the best answer to a question that lurked, half articulated in my mind. The question went like this. How can you have two local churches, at either end of the same street in the same town, of the same denomination, served by the same minister, founded about the same time, of around the same numerical size, inhabiting buildings of similar size and style, with people drawn from the same geographical region, of much the same social and economic groupings, worshipping in the same tradition – and they are as different as chalk and cheese? Any minister having pastoral charge of two or more such churches knows that is true, but why are they so different? According to the principles of much church growth theory, they shouldn't be so different at all. The same mechanistic and systemic processes should apply to both with the same expected outcomes. But they don't. It was Hopewell who, as a small part of a complicated book (written while he was dying), suggested a reason for it. Congregations are different, he proposed, because they have particular identities. Or even better, personalities. Their identity derives from their birth story and, as importantly, the story they continue to tell about themselves, articulating who they believe they are. From this story arises their identity – who they are – but also their personality – what they are like.

Our model for renewal resonates strongly with such theories of congregations. To engage with the model would be to revisit the birth story and also the continuing story through which the personality of that Christian congregation has come to be expressed. The model of renewal would not necessarily confirm the story or affirm the present congregational personality, for these might have been shaped by secondary or false birth stories and continuing self-delusion. Crucially, the model would better enable the rediscovery of the birth story in such a way that it became re-owned and retold. As a result the personality of the congregation would be reformed through a reawakened acquaintance with and retrieving of its founding charisms.

In recent years, questions of identity and purpose have bubbled to the surface of a number of debates concerning the nature of organizations and groupings. A leading voice in these debates is that of Margaret (Meg) Wheatley, an expert in organizational behaviour. I find her writing fascinating, weaving together as it does change theories and insights from what she calls 'new science' such as chaos theory. She, like Hopewell, rejects controlled mechanistic systems and suggests that organizations, such as churches – both local and denominational – are in fact living systems: 'intelligent, creative, adaptive, self-organising, and meaning-seeking'.[31] As such, 'order arises' as well as 'being imposed through direction and control.'[32] She suggests that, like many organisms, organizations will naturally self-organize and self-correct in order to be what they truly are. She writes 'Identity is the filter that every organism or system uses to make sense of the world. New information, new relationships, changing environments – all are interpreted through a sense of self . . . An organism will change to maintain its identity.'[33]

Dan Dick and Evelyn Burry ably summarize Wheatley's insights in the context of church renewal:

> When organisations begin to talk about church, they ordinarily focus on altering their structures, patterns or processes – the form the organisation takes. They decide to 'do' things differently. However, modifying behaviour is no guarantee of radical, fundamental, systemic change. Instead, real change takes place at the deeper level – the

level of our identity. The information we share identifies who we are. Our relationships – the way we put together and combine to create synergy – identify our potential. Our vision – the hopes, dreams, desires and plans that motivate and inspire us – points us in the direction we most want to go. When we spend our time reflecting on the deeper issues, changes in structures, patterns and processes automatically happen.[34]

This is precisely why our model of mission is such a potent primer for the renewal of Christian communities.

The significance of energizing

My experience is that this model for renewal energizes rather than fatigues. In a context where so many churches – locally and denominationally – appear so tired and jaded this is not an insignificant factor. One of my friends, a minister near retirement once said, 'I have spent my whole ministry in situations of decline. I have never known anything other than a move towards death.' Of course there is inherent in any model that involves 'returning' to things the danger of inviting folk who may already believe that their finest hours are past to remain there. Our model for renewal involves the past but only in the sense that it holds significant information with respect to the future of a Christian grouping. This, I find, is profoundly energizing to those who get stuck into the task.

A few years ago I spent some time with those training ministers for the Uniting Church of Australia, being a union of Congregational, Methodist and Presbyterian Churches in 1977. While there I came across a little book by Andrew Dutney, formerly a Methodist and now an ordained member of the Uniting Church. It was the title of the book that immediately caught my attention: it was called *Where Did The Joy Come From?* Dutney, like many Christians, looked round upon a Church he belonged to and recognized its exhaustion and mediocrity. There was no way, he reckoned, that hundreds of church buildings, an elaborate system of church, various structures for worship, fellowship and caring came about through the jadedness of the current church constituency. The very existence of all the trappings of a denomination signals that once, however long ago, there was vision, vitality and vigour. So where did the joy come from? This led him to a rediscovery of his roots, of the founding charisms, of the continuing call upon his Church and he was energized towards renewal. My hope is that the model of mission advocated here, will energize rather than further fatigue.

The last word goes to Leander Keck:

> It would be gross faithlessness to assume that the Christian faith, itself repeatedly renewed by the gospel, now lacks the capacity to renew the churches – as if our situation were more effective in draining off the vitality of the faith than that of our predecessors. If renewal and reform have come about in the past, there is no persuasive reason to deny that they will occur again.
>
> Indeed, I suspect that we are on the threshold of a new Christian sensibility, a different understanding of what counts in

being Christian, a new pattern of piety and
practice which reflects the unity of faith
and ethics, a changed perception of what it
means to be a faithful church.[35]

To mull over . . .

- Explore some possible meanings and
  implications of the 'orphanage' story in
  relation to your local church.

- What are the 'loud words' of Jesus for you?
  What do they say about who you 'are' under
  God as a local church?

- What do you think are the 'founding
  charisms' of your church tradition and
  the life of your local church as you have
  experienced it? Why do you think God
  'raised you up' in the first place?

- What are the 'signs of the times' that you
  want particularly to note in the light of
  the loud words of Jesus and the founding
  charisms? How will you respond to them?

- How do you think God wants you to be, as a
  church, here and now?

- In what ways, do you think, is your church 'different and distinct'? Do you think these are the right and best ways of being different and distinct in the light of the mission of God?

- What might 'non-identical reproductions' of your church look like? Are you going to commit yourself to do this?

11

Faithful Risk-taking

He is no fool who gives away what he cannot keep to gain what he cannot lose.

Jim Elliot

A lapsed Christian falls off a cliff and just manages to grab a small branch on the way down.

'Help! Is there anyone there?' he cries.

'Yes, I am here,' replies a voice.

'Who are you?'

'I am God.'

'Oh thank God,' says the lapsed Christian, 'please rescue me, I'll do anything, I'll come back to church, anything . . .'

'Do you trust me?' asks God.

'Yes, yes,' blurts the man.

'Will you obey what I ask?'

'Anything, anything,' replies the man as the branch begins to bend and break.

'Then let go of the branch,' says God.

The man is silent for a moment, then cries out, 'Is there anybody else there?'

It took me many years to realize that the opposite of faith is not doubt but faithlessness. As a result of this realization I slowly learned that faithfulness was less about wrapping up the Church and keeping it nice, warm and clean for God, and was more about being obedient and open to God the supreme missioner and evangelist. Many of the stories Jesus told speak of actions done in faith and obedience, and the consequences of faithlessness and disobedience. The sower sows and, although the harvest lies in the hands of God, he knows with certainty that not to sow anything is to guarantee there is no harvest. The one who fails to use the talents given her as the master commanded is the one who loses even what she has. The disciple who fails to go when commanded by the Lord to do so is inevitably in the wrong place and misses the miracle.

Sharing in God's mission involves taking risks in faithful obedience – as God in Jesus Christ demonstrates supremely. Risk-taking obedience is required today as the Holy Spirit prepares the way, beckoning to the Church to imitate and follow into today's challenging culture, but also one so full of gospel potential. Risk-taking inevitably heightens the possibility of failure, but it also increases the chance of achievement, and mission-shaped churches seeking renewal are more concerned to be obedient and take the risk, rather than to risk failing through not taking it. Risk-taking also increases the chance of being wrong, but again mission-minded churches open to renewal take the risk in believing that the Spirit who calls them into and accompanies them in God's mission goes before, guides and corrects. Such is the nature of faithfulness. It is by definition a risky business, but then *not* taking risks is increasingly risky. And to stand outside the purposes of the missionary God is the greatest risk of all.

As Moses neared the Red Sea, the people of Israel, fresh out of Egypt snaking behind him, he asked God for reassurance.

'God, you . . . you will part the sea for us and let us across?'

'Moses, I promised it.'

'Yes. I know. Sorry. I just wanted to make sure.'

Moses reached the side of the sea, raised his staff and stretched out his hand over the water to divide it and . . . nothing happened. Outwardly pretending nothing was amiss he said quietly to God under his breath: 'Lord, I thought you promised to part the sea for us.'

And God replied: 'I did, and I will. Set off, I'll part it when you are up to your necks.'

The greatest risks facing the Church in the West today come not, ultimately, from contemporary culture, from increasing frailty and marginalization, from secularism or even the disinterest and aggression of increasing swathes of our pluralistic society. The greatest risks facing the Church today involve entrusting itself to the God of mission and following the leading of the Spirit. The Church must decide anew whether to risk believing the gospel and choose to live by it. It must risk placing itself in the hands of its rightful owner. It must risk participating in God's mission and pursuing the kingdom. It will be incredibly hard, but it is possible, because, ultimately such a Church is one that God partners in the *missio Dei* and therefore it will not lack God's presence or resources to become what it truly is. The Holy Spirit will help us. In that is the promise of renewal.

To mull over . . .

- What risks, taken in 'faithful obedience' do you think God is calling you – and your church – to make?

- What might it mean for your church to 'risk believing the gospel and choosing to live by it'?

Notes

Introduction

1. Cited in Richard McBrien, *Ministry: A Theological, Pastoral Handbook*, Harper, 1998, p. 66.
2. Cited in Diarmuid O'Murchu, *Reclaiming Spirituality*, Gateway, 1997, p. vii.
3. See Neil Dixon, *Wonder, Love and Praise: A Companion to the Methodist Worship Book*, Epworth Press, 2003, for a comprehensive account of the book, its contents and evolution.
4. Petru Dumitriu, *To the Unknown God*, cited in Leander Keck, *The Church Confident*, Abingdon Press, 1993, unpaginated, but p. 13.

Chapter 1

1. Andrew Dutney, *Where Did the Joy Come From?*, United Church Press, Melbourne, 2001, p. 14.
2. Cited in Andrew Dutney, *Where Did the Joy Come From?*, p. 3.
3. Stephen Bevans and Roger Schroeder, *Constants in Context: a Theology of Mission for Today*, Orbis, 2004, p. 7.
4. David J. Bosch outlines such a view in Part One of *Transforming Mission: Paradigm Shifts in Theology of Mission*, Orbis, 1991. See also Johannes Blauw, *The Missionary Nature of the Church*, Lutterworth Press, 1962; W. Larkin Jr and J.F. Williams, *Mission in the New Testament*, Orbis, 1998; D. Senior and C. Stuhlmueller, *The Biblical Foundations for Mission*, SCM, 1983.
5. Cited in Rui Josgrilberg, 'The Holy Spirit and the Spirit of Globalization', a paper read at the Eleventh Oxford Institute of Methodist Theological Studies, Oxford, August 2002.

Notes

6. Cited in Robert Warren, *Building Missionary Congregations*, CHP, 1995, p. 31.
7. Howard Snyder, *Liberating the Church*, Marshalls, 1973, p. 11.
8. David J. Bosch, *Transforming Mission*, p. 390.
9. John 20.21.
10. Paul R. Stevens, *The Abolition of the Laity: Vocation, Work and Ministry in a Biblical Perspective*, Paternoster Press, 1999, p. 6.
11. Lesslie Newbigin, *The Household of God*, SCM Press, 1953, p. 143.
12. J.C. Hoekendijk, 'The Church in Missionary Thinking', *International Review of Missions*, Volume 41, 1952, p. 325.
13. David J. Bosch, *Witness to the World*, Marshall, Morgan & Scott, 1980, p. 95.

Chapter 2

1. Paul Avis, *The Anglican Understanding of the Church*, SPCK, 2000, p. 6.
2. Martin Luther, 'Seventh Mark of a True Church', cited in Timothy F. Full (ed.), *Martin Luther's Basic Theological Writings*, Fortress Press, 1989, pp. 561–2.
3. Howard Snyder, *Decoding the Church*, Baker Books, 2002, pp. 22ff.
4. This is the basic thesis applied to contemporary Catholic ecclesiology by American Catholic writer Nicholas Healy in his impressive book, *Church, World and the Christian Life*, CUP, 2000.
5. Leonardo Boff, *Ecclesiogenesis*, Collins, 1986, pp. 2ff.
6. Leonardo Boff, *Ecclesiogenesis*.
7. Ronald Inglehart, *Modernization and Postmodernization: Cultural, Economic and Political Change in 43 Societies*, Princeton University Press, 1997, p78.
8. Melba Maggay, *Transforming Society*, Regnum Lynx, 1994, p. 40.
9. Melba Maggay, *Transforming Society*, p. 40.
10. See, for example, Michael Riddell, *Threshold of the Future*, SPCK, 1997.
11. Mark Greene, 'The Great Divide: Overcoming SSD Syndrome', 5th Catherwood Lecture in Public Theology, 2001,

available at the London Institute for Contemporary Christianity website.

12. Melba Maggay, *Transforming Society*, p. 35.

13. For example, the Lausanne Movement, emerging out of major conferences organized under the aegis of the Billy Graham Organization, but coming into being formally with a conference and a 'Covenant' statement in 1974.

14. See, for example, *An Anglican-Methodist Covenant*, CHP, 2001.

15. Lesslie Newbigin, *The Household of God: Lectures on the Nature of the Church*, SCM Press, 1953. See especially the chapter 'Christ in you, the hope of glory'.

16. Newbigin was among the first to identify 'Pentecostal' as a major strand or tradition of Christianity, alongside the traditional strands of Catholic and Protestant.

17. Paul Minear, *Images of the Church in the New Testament*, Lutterworth Press, 1961.

18. For an interesting example of this see Keith Russell, *In Search of the Church: New Testament Images for Tomorrow's Congregations*, Alban Institute, 1994.

19. Donald Messer, *A Conspiracy of Goodness: Contemporary Images of Christian Mission*, Abingdon Press, 1992.

20. George Lings, lecture notes on ecclesiology for a module of a Master's Degree programme run at the Church Army College, Sheffield.

Chapter 3

1. W.A. Visser t' Hooft, *Renewal of the Church*, SCM Press, 1956, pp. 71–2.

2. Extract from 'The Weavers Reel' on the album *Ovo* by Peter Gabriel, Real World, Virgin, 2000.

3. See Susan J. White, *Christian Worship and Technological Change*, Abingdon Press, 1994, pp. 80–7, and her article 'Liturgy and Technology' in Paul Bradshaw and Bryan Spinks (eds), *Liturgy in Dialogue*, SPCK, 1993, pp. 186ff.

4. 'The Gospel as Prisoner and Liberator of Culture' first published in 1982 in *Faith and Thought* 108 and in slightly amended form in *Missionalia* 10. The essay is reproduced as the first chapter in Andrew F. Walls, *The Missionary Movement in Christian History*, T. & T. Clark/Orbis, 1996.

5. Acts 2.46, 3.1, 5.42 etc.

6. See Robert and Julia Banks, *The Church Comes Home: A*

Notes

New Base for Community and Mission, Albatross Books, 1986, for a cogent appeal for the role and value of 'home church'.

7. Though the connections are less direct than they were thought to be some decades ago, many of the elements of Christian worship – sermon, lessons, a worship leader and the like – have some kind of origins in the Jewish synagogue.

8. See Acts 16.15, 17.6, 18.1–8; Romans 16.3ff; 1 Corinthians 1.14–16, etc.

9. Abraham J. Malherbe, *Social Aspects of Early Christianity* (Second Edition), Fortress Press, 1983, p. 69.

10. J.G. Davies, *The Origin and Development of Early Christian Church Architecture*, SCM Press, 1952, p. 15.

11. Celsus, 'A True Discourse Against the Christians', c.170 AD, in Jean Comby, *How to Understand the History of Christian Mission*, SCM Press, 1996, p. 8.

12. See Amy Oden (ed.), *And You Welcomed Me: A Sourcebook of Hospitality in Early Christianity*, Abingdon Press, 2001.

13 Alan Krieder, *Worship and Evangelism in Pre-Christendom*, Grove Books, 1995, p. 20.

14. Robert Warren, *Being Human, Being Church: Spirituality and Mission in the Local Church*, Marshall Pickering, 1995, p. 9.

15. Minucius, Felix, Octavius 8:4; 9:2, in Alan Krieder, *Worship and Evangelism in Pre-Christendom*, p. 18.

16. Celtic Christianity is very popular, and much literature about it tends to be speculative. However, Douglas Dales, *Light to the Isles: Missionary Theology in Celtic and Anglo-Saxon Britain*, Lutterworth Press, 1997, is well worth reading.

17. For a detailed study of the varied nature of parishes see Anthea Jones, *A Thousand Years of the English Parish*, Weidenfeld & Nicolson, 2002.

18. Lamin Sanneh, *Translating the Message: Missionary Impact on Culture*, Orbis, 1989.

19. A fuller treatment of this theme can be found in Martyn Atkins, 'The Inside-out Church (or lessons from our great-great-grandmother)', *Epworth Review*, October 1998, pp. 23–8.

20. Martyn D. Atkins, *Preaching in a Cultural Context*, Foundery Press, 2001.

21. Robert Warren, *Being Human, Being Church*, p. 34.

22. A recurring theme in Alice Mann, *Can Our Church Live?: Redeveloping Congregations in Decline*, Alban Books, 1999.

23. Matthew 16.25.

Chapter 4

1. Cited in David Hilborn, *Picking up the Pieces*, Hodder & Stoughton, 1997, p. 5.
2. For some helpful, accessible books focusing upon aspects of contemporary culture in relation to Christianity see Michael Paul Gallagher, *Clashing Symbols: An Introduction to Faith and Culture*, Darton, Longman & Todd, 2003; Stanley Grenz, *A Primer on Postmodernism*, Eerdmans, 1996, and David Hilborn, *Picking up the Pieces*, Hodder & Stoughton, 1997.
3. Stuart Murray, *Post-Christendom,* Paternoster Press, 2004, p. 19.
4. Taken from lecture notes by Stuart Murray presented to the Master's degree programme in Emerging Church run at Cliff College, September 2006 (http://cliffpostgrad.org.uk). Also found in fuller form in Murray's book, *Church after Christendom*, Paternoster Press, 2005.
5. Philip Forgarty, *The Missing God Who is Not Missed*, Columba Press, 2003.
6. See for example, Steve Bruce, *God is Dead: Secularization in the West*, Blackwell, 2002.
7. See, for example, Grace Davie, *Religion in Britain since 1945: Believing without Belonging*, Blackwell, 1994, and Robin Gill, *The Empty Church Revisited*, Ashgate Press, 2003.
8. Clive Marsh, *Christianity in a Post-Atheist Age*, SCM Press, 2002. p. 28.
9. For a range of predictions see Grace Davie, Paul Heelas, Linda Woodhead (eds), *Predicting Religion: Christian, Secular and Alternative Futures*, Ashgate Press, 2003.

Chapter 5

1. Paul Chilcote, *The Wesleyan Tradition: A Paradigm for Renewal*, Abingdon Press, 2002, p. 26.
2. Maggie Durran, *Regenerating Local Churches*, Canterbury Press, 2006, p. 5.
3. For example, the various *Natural Church Development* books by Christian A. Schwarz use organic rather than mathematical or organisational themes throughout.
4. See, for example, Bob Jackson, *Hope for the Church: Contemporary Strategies for Growth*, CHP, 2002, and *The Road to Growth: Towards a Thriving Church*, CHP, 2005.
5. Penny Jamieson, *Living at the Edge: Sacrament and Solidar-*

ity in Leadership, Mowbray, 1997, p. 149.

6. John Burkhart, *Worship*, Westminster Press, 1982, p. 18.
7. John Drane, *Faith in a Changing Culture: Creating Churches for the Next Century*, Zondervan, 1997.
8. See Acts 17.
9. Alan Jamieson, *A Churchless Faith*, SPCK, 2002.
10. Though 'leavers' present a complex picture overall, this theme is reiterated in Alan Jamieson, Jenny McIntosh and Adrienne Thompson, *Church Leavers: Faith Journeys Five Years On*, SPCK, 2006.
11. Leander Keck, *The Church Confident*, Abingdon Press, 1993, p. 41.
12. See John Finney, *Emerging Evangelism*, Darton, Longman & Todd, 2004, pp. 28–32.
13. See Diamuid O'Murchu, *Reclaiming Spirituality*, Gateway, 1997.
14. Martyn Atkins, *Preaching in a Cultural Context*, Foundery Press, 2001. p. 70.
15. See Michael Green, *After Alpha*, Kingsway, 2004, for a consideration of these issues.
16. See Richard Steele (ed.), *Heart Religion in the Methodist Tradition and Related Movements*, Scarecrow Press, 2001, Chapter 2.
17. Clive Marsh, in conversation arising from points made in his book, *Christianity in a Post-Atheist Age*, SCM Press, 2002, pp. 105–12.
18. See, for example, Peter Toon, *About Turn: The Decisive Event of Conversion*, Hodder & Stoughton, 1987, especially Chapter 7.
19. 1 Corinthians 3.6
20. R. Kew and R. White, *New Millennium, New Church*, Cowley, 1992, p. 110.

Chapter 6

1. Tim Chester, lecture on Church Planting, Master's Degree Programme in Mission and Evangelism, Cliff College.
2. There is evidence to support these assertions. Peter Brierley and Heather Wraight have produced material through the Christian Research Institute for many years and recent publications provide some evidence for both the move to larger and smaller congregations in England.
3. For example, the *average* membership of a Methodist Church

in Great Britain is about 30–40 members.

4. The 'mega-church' has been much vaunted and its absence from Britain sometimes rued. The best account and assessment of such churches remains George Hunter's book, *Church for the Unchurched*, Abingdon Press, 1996. It is clear that in spite of the high profile huge churches have, even in the USA they remain a rare expression of church in proportion to the churchgoing population.

5. See, for example, the material collected and analysed by Mark Greene in *The Three-eared Preacher: A Listening Tool for Busy Ministers*, London Bible College, 1998.

6. Yves Congar, *Lay People in the Church: A Study for a Theology of Laity*, Christian Classics, 1985, p. 324.

7. See, for example, William Beckham, *The Second Reformation: Reshaping the Church for the 21st Century*, Touch Publications, 1995.

8. This point is also made by Alan Jamieson in *A Churchless Faith*, SPCK, 2002.

9. Some helpful material exists. Though pretty old now Martin Robinson and Dan Yarnell's *Celebrating the Small Church*, Monarch, 1993, repays reading. Very recently published material from CHP's *Mission-shaped Church* series promises to be a good-quality resource.

10. Terry Pratchett, *Small Gods*, Gollancz, 1992, p. 281.

11. Vicky Cosstick, a lecture on the Consultancy Mission and Ministry Master's degree programme at Cliff College, and alluded to in her contribution to *Parish Project: Resource Book for Parishes to Review their Mission*, HarperCollins, 2002.

12. Sue Knight, *NLP at Work*, Nicholas Brealey Publishing, 2002.

13. 'Faith in Life', the National Church Life Survey 2001, produced by Churches Information for Mission (now disbanded).

14. Bob Jackson, *The Road to Growth*, CHP, 2005, p. 65.

15. *International Review of Mission*, vol. LXXXVI, no. 342, July 1997, p. 210.

16. Susan Rooke-Matthews, a letter to *The Friend*, vol. 151, 1993, p. 953.

17. Graham Tomlin, *The Provocative Church*, SPCK, 2004, p. 105.

18. Michael Riddell, *Threshold of the Future*, SPCK, 1997, p. 169.

Notes

19. An interview with Paul Chambers, recorded for a Master's dissertation, 2002.
20. John A.T. Robinson, *The New Reformation*, SCM Press, 1965, p. 92.
21. Diarmuid O'Murchu, *Reclaiming Spirituality*, Gateway, 1997, p. 162.
22. Avery Dulles, *Models of the Church* (expanded edition), Bantam Doubleday, 1991.
23. Avery Dulles, *Models of the Church*, p. 89.
24. See, for example, Timothy Yates' book, *Christian Mission in the Twentieth Century*, CUP, 1994.
25. Andrew Dutney, *Where Did the Joy Come From?*, United Church Press, Melbourne, 2001, p. 18.
26. Based on a story by Ann Morisy told at Cliff College some years ago.
27. See Mike Frost and Alan Hirsch, *The Shaping of Things to Come: Innovation and Mission for the 21st Century Church*, Hendrickson Publishers, 2003.

Chapter 7

1. Marcus Minucius Felix, *Octavius*, 31.7; 38.5.
2. Diarmuid O'Murchu, *Our World in Transition*, Book Guild Ltd, 1992, p. 79.
3. See, for example, Jonathan Bonk, *Missions and Money: Affluence as a Western Missionary Problem*, Orbis, 1992. Jan Nendick, a Master's student at Cliff College some years ago, discovered that invested income was a key factor in mission atrophy in local churches.
4. Hugh Price Hughes Lectures 2002, delivered at and published by Hinde Street Methodist Church (West London Methodist Mission) pp. 21–2.
5. Heather Wraight, *Eve's Glue: The Role Women Play in Holding the Church Together*, Paternoster Lifestyle/Christian Research, 2001, p.11, but a major theme through the whole book.
6. Heather Wraight, *Eve's Glue*, Chapters 1 and 6.
7. Penny Jamieson, *Living at the Edge: Sacrament and Solidarity in Leadership*, Mowbray, 1997, p. 152.
8. Bryant Myers, 'Women and Mission', *MARC Newsletter*, no. 93–93, September 1993.
9. See John Finney, *Finding Faith Today: How Does it Happen?*, Bible Society, 1992.

10. John Finney, *Emerging Evangelism*, Darton, Longman & Todd, 2004, p. 136.
11. *Mission-shaped Church*, CHP, 2004.
12. Robert Warren, *Being Human, Being Church: Spirituality and Mission in the Local Church*, Marshall Pickering, 1995, p. 95.
13. Anthea Jones, *A Thousand Years of the English Parish*, Weidenfeld & Nicolson, 2002, p. 287.
14. Leslie Francis and Philip Richter, *Gone but not Forgotten: Church Leaving and Returning*, Darton, Longman & Todd, 1998.
15. Anthea Jones, *A Thousand Years of the English Parish*.
16. *Breaking New Ground: Church Planting in the Church of England*, CHP, 1994.
17. See, for example, Nick Spencer, *Parochial Vision: the Future of the English Parish*, Paternoster Press, 2004.
18. Christopher Walker, *Seeking Relevant Churches for the 21ˢᵗ Century*, JBCE Books, Melbourne, 1997, p. 117.
19. Robert Warren, *Being Human, Being Church,* p. 169.
20. Thomas Weiser (ed.), *Planning for Mission*, Epworth Press, 1966, pp. 10–11.
21. Ulrich Beck, *What is Globalization?*, Polity Press, 2000, p. 74.
22. Roland Allen, *Missionary Methods: St Paul's or Ours?*, Lutterworth Press, 2006 (first published 1912).
23. Donald McGavran, *The Bridges of God: A Study in the Strategy of Missions*, Friendship Press, 1955, p. 23.
24. Donald McGavran, in C. Peter Wagner (ed.), *Understanding Church Growth*, Eerdmans, 1990, p. 163.
25. Galatians, 3.28.
26. Robert Warren, *Being Human, Being Church,* p. 27.
27. Ann Morisy, *Journeying Out: A New Approach to Christian Mission*, Continuum, 2004, p. 7.
28. Ann Morisy, *Journeying Out,* p. 45.
29. Ann Morisy, *Journeying Out,* p. 54.
30. Ann Morisy, *Journeying Out,* p. 58.
31. Ann Morisy, *Journeying Out,* p. 23.
32. Ann Morisy, *Journeying Out,* pp. 183–4.
33. Lesslie Newbigin, *The Gospel in a Pluralist Society*, SPCK, 1989, p. 227.
34. Gregory Jones and Michael Cartwright, 'Vital Congregations', in Alan Padgett (ed.), *The Mission of the Church in Methodist Perspective: The World is my Parish*, Edwin Mellen Press, 1993, p. 112.

35. Gregory Jones and Michael Cartwright, 'Vital Congregations', p. 113.
36. Stanley Hauerwas and William Willimon, *Resident Aliens: Life in the Christian Colony*, Abingdon Press, 1989, p. 27.
37. Robert Bellah, *Habits of the Heart*, University of California Press, 1985, pp. 71–5.
38. Gregory Jones and Michael Cartwright, 'Vital Congregations', p. 113.
39. Gregory Jones and Michael Cartwright, 'Vital Congregations', pp. 113–14.
40. Richard Keyes, *Chameleon or Tribe? Recovering Authentic Christian Community*, IVP, 1999.

Chapter 8

1. Mike Riddell, an interview with Paul Chambers, 2002.
2. Sheldon Vanauken, *A Severe Mercy*, Bantam Books, 1981, p. 82.
3. Rebecca Manley Pippert, *Out of the Saltshaker: Evangelism as a Way of Life*, IVP, 1979, p. 16.
4. See Gavin Reid, *To Reach a Nation: The Challenge of Evangelism in a Mass-media Age*, Hodder & Stoughton, 1987.
5. See John Finney, *Recovering the Past*, Darton, Longman & Todd, 1996, pp. 37ff., and his *Emerging Evangelism*, Darton, Longman & Todd, 2004, pp. 70ff.
6. See House of Bishops, *Good News People*, CHP, 1999.
7. For a clear outline of what evangelism is and is not, see Michael Green, *Evangelism through the Local Church*, Hodder & Stoughton, 1990, Chapter 1.
8. See Martyn Atkins, 'More than Words? Christian Apologetics for a new Millennium', in *A Charge to Keep*, compiled by Brian Thornton, Methodist Publishing House, 1999, pp. 68–75.
9. Brian McLaren, *More Ready Than You Realize: Evangelism as Dance in the Postmodern Matrix*, Zondervan, 2002, p. 27.
10. Brian McLaren, *More Ready Than You Realize*, p. 29.
11. William Abraham, *The Logic of Evangelism*, Eerdmans, 1989, p. 95.
12. This section is presented as an article 'From Darkness to Light – lessons in disciple-making from our great-grandparents in Christ', published in Mark Greene and Tracy Cotterell (eds), *Let My People Grow*, Authentic Publishing, 2006, pp. 57–69.

13. David Watson, *Discipleship,* Hodder & Stoughton, 1981, p. 18.
14. One of the best accounts of ancient catechesis is Thomas M. Finn, *From Death to Rebirth: Ritual and Conversion in Antiquity,* Paulist Press, 1997.
15. A helpful outline of these stages is found in C. Jones, G. Wainwright, E. Yarnold and P. Bradshaw (eds), *The Study of Liturgy*, SCM Press, 1992, pp. 127ff.
16. This is illustrated wonderfully in Alan Krieder, *The Change of Conversion and the Origin of Christendom,* Trinity Press International, 1999.
17. Martin Robinson, *The Faith of the Unbeliever,* Monarch, 1994, p. 93.
18. See William Abraham, *The Logic of Evangelism,* especially Chapter 1.
19. A helpful overview of contemporary approaches to initiation is the Church of England Report, *On the Way,* CHP, 1995.
20. John Finney, *Finding Faith Today: How Does it Happen?,* British and Foreign Bible Society, 1992.
21. Philip Richter and Leslie Francis, *Gone but not Forgotten: Church Leaving and Returning,* Darton Longman & Todd, 1998. See Chapter 2 particularly.
22. See, for example, the work of Jim Fowler, especially *Stages of Faith*, HarperCollins, 1995, and *Becoming Adult, Becoming Christian*, Harper & Row, 1984.

Chapter 9

1. Walter Brueggemann, 'Covenanting as Human Vocation', *Interpretation* 33:2 (April), 1979, p. 126.
2. T.W. Gillespie, 'The Laity in Biblical Perspective', *Theology Today* 36:3 (October), 1979, p. 327.
3. Michael Green, *Evangelism in the Early Church*, Hodder & Stoughton, 1970.
4. Bob Jackson, *The Road to Growth*, CHP, 2005, p. 141.
5. From a study by Georgia Harkness, *The Church and Its Laity*, Abingdon Press, 1962, pp. 15–16, recorded in Paul Stevens, *The Abolition of the Laity*, Paternoster Press, 2000, p. 25.
6. *Studying The Making of Ministry: A Study Guide to the Report 'The Making of Ministry'*, The Methodist Publishing House, January 1997, (unpaginated, but effectively p. 5).
7. Howard Snyder (ed.), *Global Good News: Mission in a New Context*, chapter 'The Gospel as Global Good News' (by

Howard Snyder), Abingdon Press, 2001, p. 230.

8. A phrase used by Paul Stevens (among others) in a book of that title.

9. See R. Kew and R. White, *New Millennium, New Church*, Cowley, 1992, pp. 134ff., for a fuller account of 'Boomers' in relation to church belonging.

10. R. Kew and R. White, *New Millennium, New Church*, p. 85.

11. Diarmuid O' Murchu, *Reclaiming Spirituality*, Gateway Press, 1997, p. 29.

12. Mary Daly, *Gyn/Ecology*, Beacon Press, 1978, pp. 30ff. Summarized in O' Murchu, *Reclaiming Spirituality*, pp. 102–3.

13. John A.T. Robinson, *On Being the Church in the World*, Pelican Books, 1969, pp.89–90.

14. Alvin Tofler, *The Third Wave*, cited in Robert Warren, *Being Human, Being Church*, Marshall Pickering, 1995, p. 93.

15. Bob Jackson, *The Road to Growth*, p. 145.

16. Based on a list in Bob Jackson, *The Road to Growth*, p. 121.

17. Leander Keck, *The Church Confident*, Abingdon Press, 1993, pp. 93–4.

18. Tony Benn, in a speech in 1983, and repeated many times thereafter.

19. Steven Croft, *Transforming Communities*, Darton, Longman & Todd, 2002, p. 28.

20. Paul Stevens, *The Abolition of the Laity*, p. 19.

Chapter 10

1. Carl G. Jung, *On the Nature and Activity of the Psyche*, CWIH, para. 505.

2. Loosely based on a reference to a consultancy Alice Mann undertook. See Alice Mann, *Can Our Church Live? Redeveloping Congregations in Decline*, Alban Books, 1999, pp. 22–3.

3. C. Jamieson, *To Live is to Change: A way of Reading Vatican II*, Rejoice Publications, 1995, p. 77.

4. Listed by George Lovell in correspondence, February 2002, itself shaped by material supplied to Lovell by Sister Margaret O'Connor (a member and one time provincial of the Order Daughters of the Holy Spirit). See also Pope Paul VI letter *Ecclesiae Sanctae* on *The Renewal of Religious Life*, articles 5, 11, 17–20, 31 and 51–5.

5. Luke 4.18.
6. Doris Donnelly (ed.), *Retrieving Charisms for the Twenty-first Century*, Liturgical Press, 1999, p. ix.
7. See, for example, R.D. Urlin, *The Churchman's Life of Wesley*, SPCK, 1880.
8. See, for example, J.H. Rigg, *The Living Wesley*, Charles Kelly, 1891, or much more recently Howard Snyder, *The Radical Wesley: Pattern for Church Renewal*, Zondervan, 1987.
9. See, for example, Frank Baker, *A Charge to Keep*, Epworth Press, 1947, pp. 101–42, in which 'what Methodism stands for' is outlined in nine themes, or Rupert E. Davies, *Methodism*, Epworth Press, second revised edition, 1985, pp. 11ff., in which 'dominant characteristics' are outlined.
10. For example, Arthur Skevington Wood, *The Burning Heart: John Wesley, Evangelist*, Cliff College Publishing, 2001 (first published in 1976 by Paternoster Press).
11. Paul Chilcote (ed.), *The Wesleyan Tradition*, Abingdon Press, 2002, p. 35.
12. Laceye Warner, 'Offer Them Christ', in Paul Chilcote (ed.), *The Wesleyan Tradition*, p. 163.
13. Gregory Jones and Michael Cartwright, 'Vital Congregations' in Alan Padgett (ed), *The Mission of the Church in Methodist Perspective: The World is my Parish*, Edwin Mellen Press, 1993, p. 111.
14. Précised from Donnelly (ed.), *Retrieving Charisms for the Twenty-first Century*, pp. ix–x.
15. 'Charisms: an ecclesiological exploration', in Donnelly (ed.), *Retrieving Charisms for the Twenty-first Century*, p. 2.
16. Robin Greenwood, *Transforming Church*, SPCK, 2002, p. 27–8.
17. Cited in David Oakley, *Pastoral Ministry: An Essay in Pastoral Theology*, Pentland Books, 2001, p. 55.
18. Cited in David Oakley, *Pastoral Ministry*, p. 55.
19. Lesslie Newbigin, *Proper Confidence: Faith, Doubt and Certainty in Christian Discipleship*, SPCK, 1995, p. 38.
20. See, for example, Alice Mann, *Can Our Church Live?* pp. 3ff.
21. Antonio Romano, *The Charism of the Founder: The Person and Charism of Founders in Contemporary Theological Reflection*, St Paul's, 1994, p. 23.
22. Antonio Romano, *The Charism of the Founder*, p. 20.
23. Antonio Romano, *The Charism of the Founder*, p. 20
24. Antonio Romano, *The Charism of the Founder*, p. 21.

Notes

25. Antonio Romano, *The Charism of the Founder*, p. 20.
26. Type the phrase into 'Google' and see where it takes you!
27. Alice Mann, *Can Our Church Live?*, p. 1.
28. See, for example, Howard Snyder, *Decoding the Church: Mapping the DNA of Christ's Body*, Baker Books, 2002.
29. Eddie Gibbs, *Followed or Pushed?* MARC Europe, 1987.
30. James Hopewell, *Congregation: Stories and Structures*, Augsberg Fortress, 1987.
31. Margaret Wheatley and Myron Kellner-Rogers, A *Simpler Way*, Berrett-Koehler Publications, 1996, p. 3.
32. Scott London, 'The New Science of Leadership: An interview with Margaret Wheatley', available at: www.scottlondon. com
33. Margaret Wheatley and Myron Kellner-Rogers, A *Simpler Way*, p. 14.
34. Dan Dick and Evelyn Berry, *Quest: a Journey Towards a New Kind of Church*, Discipleship Resources, 2003, pp. 70–71.
35. Leander Keck, *The Church Confident*, Abingdon Press, 1993, p. 19.

A few ideas for further reading . . .

Mission-shaped Church, CHP, 2004.

William Abraham, *The Logic of Evangelism*, Eerdmans, 1989.

Paul Bayes and Tim Sledge, *Mission-shaped Parish*, CHP, 2006.

Stephen Cottrell, *From the Abundance of the Heart*, Darton, Longman & Todd, 2006.

Steven Croft, *Transforming Communities*, Darton, Longman & Todd, 2002.

John Finney, *Emerging Evangelism*, Darton, Longman & Todd, 2004.

Michael Frost and Alan Hirsch, *The Shape of Things to Come*, Hendrickson, 2003.

Eddie Gibbs and Ryan Bolger, *Emerging Churches*, Baker, 2006

Richard Giles, *Re-pitching the Tent*, Canterbury Press, 2004.

Susan Hope, *Mission-shaped Spirituality*, CHP, 2006.

Bob Jackson, *The Road to Growth*, CHP, 2005.

Alice Mann, *Can Our Church Live?*, Alban Books, 1999.

Brian McLaren, *More Ready Than You Realize*, Zondervan, 2002.

Ann Morisy, *Journeying Out*, Continuum, 2004.

Michael Moynagh, *emergingchurch.intro*, Monarch, 2004.

Stuart Murray, *Church after Christendom*, Paternoster Press, 2005.

Mike Riddell, *Threshold of the Future*, SPCK, 1997.

Wolfgang Simson, *Houses That Change the World*, OM Publishing, 2001.

Nick Spencer, *Parochial Vision*, Paternoster Press, 2004.

Paul Stevens, *The Abolition of the Laity*, Paternoster Press, 1999.